Finding Jesus *in the* *Book of* Revelation

A Participant's
Guide to a
10-session Study
of the Book of
Revelation

© 2012, 2014 by Steve Case and Daniel Wysong
Published by Involve Youth, P.O. Box 2424, Carmichael, CA 95609
Printed in the United States of America
All rights reserved

Edited by Chris Blake
Designed by Kari McKinney

The authors assume full responsibility for the accuracy of all facts and
quotations as cited in this book.

You can obtain additional copies of this book by visiting
www.Revelation101.com.

Unless otherwise indicated, all Scripture texts are taken from the
HOLY BIBLE, NEW INTERNATIONAL VERSION® NIV®. Copyright ©
1973, 1978, 1984, 2011 by Biblica, Inc.® Used by permission of Biblica,
Inc.® All rights reserved worldwide.

Scriptures quoted from KJV are from the King James Version.

Scripture quotations marked NLT are taken from the Holy Bible, New
Living Translation, copyright © 1996, 2004. Used by permission of Tyndale
House Publishers, Inc., Wheaton, Illinois 60189. All rights reserved.

Scriptures quoted from TLB are from The Living Bible, copyright © 1971.
Used by permission of Tyndale House Publishers, Inc., Wheaton, Illinois
60189. All rights reserved.

Scripture quotation from The Message. Copyright © by Eugene H. Peterson,
1993, 1994, 1995, 1996, 2000, 2001, 2002. Used by permission of
NavPress Publishing Group.

Scriptures marked NCV quoted from The Holy Bible, New Century Version,
copyright 1987, 1988, 1991 by Word Publishing, a division of Thomas
Nelson, Inc. Used by permission.

Scripture quoted from NASB are from The New American Standard Bible®,
Copyright © 1960, 1962, 1963, 1968, 1971, 1972, 1973, 1975, 1977, 1995
by the Lockman Foundation. Used by permission.

Case, Steve, 1957–
Finding Jesus in the Book of Revelation (Participant's Guide),
by Steve Case and Daniel Wysong.

ISBN 13: 978-0-9850097-2-4 (paperback)
ISBN 10: 0985009721 (paperback)

12 13 14 15 • 5 4 3 2

How to Use This Guide

This is your study guide for *Revelation 101: Finding Jesus in the Book of Revelation*. Put your name on the front cover. Mark up the inside. Take notes in the spaces provided. Write out questions you want to discuss later. Make this your own resource!

Some pages have lots of space for writing, and other pages simply provide additional information for your future use or if you want to look a little deeper into one of the topics that gets covered. Your Bible study leader might have made some adjustments to the content you cover, perhaps emphasizing one element a little more or breezing over something else. Don't blame your leader for sensing a need to improve these materials. Thank your leader! We hope that you and your presenter will continue to grow in your relationship with Jesus, just as the seminar creators continue to do.

This *Participant's Guide* is not a "stand alone" study. You should use it in conjunction with a leader who has the *Presenter's Manual*. Otherwise, some pages in your *Participant's Guide* will appear to have too many blanks. Another page might seem out of context without the leader's presentation that explains that page. If you want more information regarding materials related to *Revelation 101: Finding Jesus in the Book of Revelation*, go to www.Revelation101.com.

Our prayer for you is that your relationship with Jesus will increase in passion, deepen in trust, and provide the endurance you need as you live for God on this earth in anticipation of Christ's soon return.

How This Got Started

What draws you to the Book of Revelation? Some have grown up with lots of exposure and some know very little about the book. Sensational tidbits such as "Armageddon" or "666" or "beasts" or "flying horsemen" or "144,000" provide fodder for wild imaginations and outlandish predictions. Some feel a jolt of fervor when they hear a new announcement regarding Revelation. Others have burned out and feel hardened if someone broaches the topic. And still others are simply curious. What about you? What draws you to the Book of Revelation?

We are two pastors who grew up hearing the prophecies of Revelation, but our focus had changed to other parts of Scripture. Then a church member in a small group Bible study asked that the group begin a study in the book of Revelation. Others supported the idea. After getting over our initial avoidance of the topic, we began in earnest to take a fresh look at the book of Revelation. Instead of following an established school of interpretation for Revelation, we wanted to see what the book had to say on its own terms. Bible scholars call this "exegesis." Others would say it's understanding the Bible by looking into the text to uncover what the Bible writers initially communicated, and then applying that to our day.

What we found amazed and overwhelmed us. Maybe we hadn't listened very well before. Recent scholarship revealed so much more to us. Three scholars in particular caught our attention: Jon Paulien, Ranko Stefanovic, and Jacques Doukhan. What they have published shows remarkable similarity, and yet they are not identical. We considered other sources as well, but these three became our "go to" sources for understanding Revelation in a fresh way. It truly became "the revelation of Jesus Christ" for us!

This renewed immersion into Revelation made its impact on us. First of all we are amazed by Jesus—more than ever! We want to share Him with others, and we are committed to discovering more. We also pray what you find in your own study will take you beyond where you are.

We called this *Revelation 101* because we are targeting people who are able to think at the level of a college introduction course—101. This isn't for Vacation Bible School or merely rote memorization. Yet in calling this an introductory course, we want people to keep going. We have found that high school students capable of focused thinking appreciate this material. The subtitle *Finding Jesus in the Book of Revelation* helps maintain our focus on Jesus instead of the dragon or beasts or persecution. This focus enables us to stay true to the first verse of Revelation: "The revelation of Jesus Christ."

After presenting *Revelation101: Finding Jesus in the Book of Revelation* in our local church, we revised the material so small group Bible study leaders as well as pastors could present this in seminar format. May your study lead you into a deeper relationship with the Jesus revealed here.

Steve Case, *President*
INVOLVE YOUTH

Daniel Wysong, *Lead Pastor*
CHICO SEVENTH-DAY ADVENTIST CHURCH

What Others Are Saying About
Revelation 101: Finding Jesus in the Book of Revelation

"One of the church's greatest needs is to frame its prophetic vision in terms attractive and understandable to youth. This is the best such attempt I have seen."

Jon Paulien, *Revelation Scholar*
DEAN, LOMA LINDA UNIVERSITY SCHOOL OF RELIGION
AUTHOR OF *REVELATION–HOPE, MEANING, PURPOSE*

~~~~~

"Our church finds its mission in the heart of Revelation. *Revelation 101* provides an ideal resource for churches and Bible study groups to explore Revelation and to see that it is indeed the "Revelation of Jesus Christ."

Jim Pedersen, *President*
NORTHERN CALIFORNIA CONFERENCE OF SEVENTH-DAY ADVENTISTS

~~~~~

"This concise exposition of the last book of the Bible offers enough fresh insights to provoke the reader's interest in reading it. Its clear writing and practical style will appeal both to pastors and lay-Bible students looking for more practical application of the Revelation's text. The book proves to be an excellent resource for preaching and teaching as well as for small groups studying the Book of Revelation. "

Ranko Stefanovic, *Professor of New Testament*
ANDREWS UNIVERSITY SEVENTH-DAY ADVENTIST
THEOLOGICAL SEMINARY
AUTHOR OF THE COMMENTARY *REVELATION OF JESUS CHRIST*

~~~~~

"This practical and biblical seminar series on the book of Revelation is a great tool and guide that forges one through the decline of all human systems and dominions to focus on Jesus Christ, the King of Kings and Lord of Lords."

Ivan L. Williams, Sr., *Ministerial Director*
NORTH AMERICA DIVISION OF SEVENTH-DAY ADVENTISTS

"The Book of Revelation is probably the most difficult book of the Bible, and perhaps the most unpopular and dangerous. These lessons are clear, engaging, and interesting, bringing to the public the great hope that is so needed in our days of troubles."

Jacques Doukhan, *Professor of Hebrew and Old Testament Exegesis*
ANDREWS UNIVERSITY SEVENTH-DAY ADVENTIST
THEOLOGICAL SEMINARY
AUTHOR OF *SECRETS OF REVELATION*

~~~

Revelation 101 is a resource I've wanted for a long time! As an Academy Bible teacher I am thrilled to finally be able to use a resource that gets to the heart of what the Book of Revelation is all about: the revelation of Jesus Christ. This is something we need in these last days, especially with our students.

Krystalynn Martin, *Pastor and Bible Teacher*
RIO LINDO ADVENTIST ACADEMY

~~~

"When our congregation wanted to reach out to our community with our understanding of Jesus Christ, we found *Revelation 101: Finding Jesus in the Book of Revelation* to be the ideal conduit for sharing this. Not surprisingly, our own congregation benefitted tremendously as well!"

Keith Jacobson, *Lead Pastor*
CARMICHAEL SEVENTH-DAY ADVENTIST CHURCH

Table of Contents

"The Revelation of Jesus Christ..."

Revelation 1:1

Introduction and Four Keys for Interpreting Revelation

Basic Outline

Intro: "The Revelation of Jesus Christ"

A. **Schools of Interpretation.**

   1. *The Past (Preterist).* Revelation is a history of the first century AD.

   2. *The Future (Futurist).* Revelation describes the future and we can discover it.

   3. *History (Historicist).* Revelation describes the span of history from the early Christian Church until Christ's Second Coming.

   4. *Spiritual (Symbolic or Idealist).* Personal applications from the Book of Revelation.

B. **Keys for a Bible Explanation of Revelation.**

   1. *Key 1 – Literary Context.* Reading in context—check before and after.

   2. *Key 2 – Historical Context.* Get familiar with that time and culture.

   3. *Key 3 – Key Words.* Some words in the text are pregnant with meaning.

   4. *Key 4 – Compare With Other Scripture.* Some parts of the Bible illuminate other parts.

C. **Summary Statement:** These first four keys are for any book of the Bible.

D. Next Session: Three keys unique to Revelation.

While there might be considerable differences between various interpretations of the Book of Revelation, they pretty much boil down to four major schools of interpretation. Each of these utilizes the Bible but follows a different interpretation and arrives at different understandings. Any school of interpretation can be used consistently throughout the entire Book of Revelation, although it might fit more easily in some places than in others. Mixing schools of interpretation can be confusing. Here is a brief explanation of each of the four major schools of interpretation with the Book of Revelation.

Past (or Preterist) – what John wrote relates to the past, not the future. The messages given in Revelation were for the first century Christian Church, including the fall of Jerusalem in AD 70 and the persecution of early Christians by both Romans and Jews. Mainline Protestants and Catholics fit into this school.

Future (or Futurist) – most of the events described in Revelation will take place in the future. The secret rapture of the church starts this, followed by a seven-year period of "tribulation" (based primarily on one verse in Daniel 9) in which Jews will come to follow Jesus as the Messiah. Many evangelicals, TV preachers, and the popular *Left Behind* novels adhere to this school.

History (or Historicist) – starts with the early Christian church and spans the rest of earth's history, ending with Christ's Second Coming. This was the Protestant interpretation during the Reformation. Few people consistently and exclusively hold to this today, although it is the school the Seventh-day Adventist Church follows to a great extent.

Spiritual (or Idealist or Symbolic) – a personal application based on the major conflict between good and evil that keeps repeating itself so it relates to Christians in any age. Mainline Protestants, mystics, those not interested in time-related prophecies, and those looking for personal applications prefer this school.

Following are two verses from Revelation, and how these two verses can be interpreted simply by using a different school of interpretation.

Revelation 6:1-2 – "I watched as the Lamb opened the first of the seven seals. Then I heard one of the four living creatures say in a voice like thunder, 'Come!' I looked, and there before me was a white horse! Its rider held a bow, and he was given a crown, and he rode out as a conqueror bent on conquest."

Four Schools of Interpretation for These Verses

Past (or Preterist) – The white horse symbolizes the Roman leader, Titus, who is bringing judgment on the apostate city, Jerusalem, that killed the prophets and then the Messiah. He will conquer Jerusalem as part of God's vengeance against evil.

Future (or Futurist) – A white horse usually would be considered to be good. Don't be fooled! This isn't Christ, but the Antichrist, going out to conquer the earth. This happens after God's people have been secretly raptured to heaven. This Antichrist is the same as the terrible sea beast of Revelation 13.

History (or Historicist) – White horse symbolizes good. The bow indicates the rider is armed, going out on conquest. This symbolizes the initial surge of taking the Gospel to the world in the first century AD.

Spiritual (or Idealist or Symbolic) – God rides victoriously. Whoever rules as a king or national leader does so only because God has placed that person there, and God can take that same person down—as evidenced throughout the course of history.

Four Schools of Interpretation for Revelation

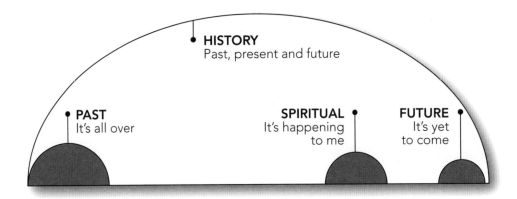

HISTORY
Past, present and future

PAST
It's all over

SPIRITUAL
It's happening
to me

FUTURE
It's yet
to come

The First Four Keys for Explaining Revelation

1. Literary Context

   What before and after verses say.

2. Historical/Cultural Context

   John on island Patmos because of word of God and testimony of Jesus. Christians were not bending knees to Romans. Jews started out punishing Christians & were protected by Romans. Then Romans started persecuting Christians

   Goddess Hekate holds keys heaven or hell

3. Key Words

   95 AD   7 churches in Turkey

   Rev 1:1 Revelation Made it known, signified it, simplified it

4. Compare With Other Scripture

   Rev 1: 4-5

   7 spirits

SESSION 1

Revelation 1:1 *in symbols*   *so Romans would not understand.*

King James Version and New King James Version
The Revelation of Jesus Christ, which God gave unto him to show unto his servants things which must shortly come to pass; and he sent and **signified** it by his angel unto his servant John.

New International Version
The revelation from Jesus Christ, which God gave him to show his servants what must soon take place. He **made it known** by sending his angel to his servant John.

New Living Translation
This is a revelation from Jesus Christ, which God gave him concerning the events that will happen soon. An angel was sent to God's servant John so that John could **share the revelation** with God's other servants.

New Century Version
This is the revelation of Jesus Christ, which God gave to him to show his servants what must soon happen. And Jesus sent his angel to **show** it to his servant John.

The Message
A revealing of Jesus, the Messiah. God gave it to make plain to his servants what is about to happen. He **published** and delivered it by Angel to his servant John.

New American Standard Bible
The Revelation of Jesus Christ, which God gave him to show to his bond-servants the things which must soon take place; and He sent and **communicated** it by His angel to His bond-servant John.

The Living Bible
This book unveils some of the future activities soon to occur in the life of Jesus Christ. God permitted him to reveal these things to his servant John in a vision; and then an angel was sent from heaven to **explain** the vision's meaning.

The Greek word is *"semaino"* which means to signify, to give a sign, indicate, expressing by signs. See also John 12:33; 18:32; 21:19.

Seven Spirits of God

Revelation 1:4-5 – "the seven spirits before his throne" with "him who is, and who was, and who is to come" (God the Father) with "Jesus Christ, who is the faithful witness, the firstborn from the dead, and the ruler of the kings of the earth."

Revelation 5:6 – The Lamb (Jesus) is presented as having "seven horns and seven eyes, which are the seven spirits of God sent out into all the earth." (See Zechariah 4:10 for seven lamps which are the eyes of the Lord that range through the earth [He sees everything and knows everything]. See also John 16:12-15 regarding Jesus going to heaven and sending the Spirit to earth in his place.)

Isaiah 11:2 – The Spirit of the Lord will rest on him (the stump of Jesse, David's father)—the Spirit of wisdom and of understanding, the Spirit of counsel and of might, the Spirit of the knowledge and fear of the Lord. Numbering these yields the following:

1. The Spirit of the Lord
2. The Spirit of Wisdom
3. The Spirit of Understanding
4. The Spirit of Counsel
5. The Spirit of Might
6. The Spirit of Knowledge
7. The Spirit of the Fear of the Lord

The seven spirits get associated with God the Father (the OT Yahweh) and God the Son (Jesus). From a Christian belief of the Trinity (Father, Son, and Holy Spirit) the obvious reference of the seven spirits is God the Holy Spirit.

Three More Keys for Interpreting Revelation

Basic Outline

Intro: Review the four schools of interpretation.

A. Review: The first four keys for a Bible Explanation of Revelation.

1. *Key 1 – Literary Context.*   Rev 20: *Unveiling of Jesus through symbols of the Old testament*

2. *Key 2 – Historical Context.*   *90-95 AD*

3. *Key 3 – Key Words.*

4. *Key 4 – Compare with the Rest of Scripture.*

B. **Keys for a Bible Explanation of Revelation** (Continued).

1. *Key 5 – Check for Old Testament Roots.*

2. *Key 6 – Jesus Changes Everything.* Jesus is the answer to OT/NT.

3. *Key 7 – Structure in the Book of Revelation.*

   a. Parallels.

   b. Numbers are symbolic. 7

   c. Pyramid/chiastic structure

C. **Summary Statement:** The seven keys for interpreting Revelation.

The First Four

1. Literary Context

   _____

   _____

2. Historical/Cultural Context

   _____

   _____

3. Key Words

   _____

   _____

4. Compare With Other Scripture

   _____

   _____

Three More

5. Look for Old Testament Roots

   _____

   _____

6. Jesus Changes Everything
   (OT fulfilled by Jesus; NT flows from Jesus)

   _____

   _____

7. Structure in the Book of Revelation

   _____

   _____

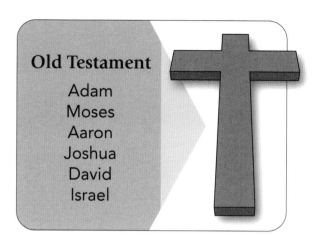

SESSION 2

Jesus Changes Everything!

What was *literal* in the OT becomes spiritual/symbolic in the NT. What was *local* in the OT becomes global in the NT.

Literal to Spiritual/Symbolic

Literal "Children of Israel" become spiritual/symbolic

_____

Literal "animal sacrifices" become spiritual/symbolic

_____

Literal "King David" becomes spiritual/symbolic

_____

Literal "blood on the doorposts for Passover" becomes spiritual/symbolic

_____

Local to Global

What was locally "Jerusalem" in the OT becomes globally

_____

What was locally "the temple" in the OT becomes globally

_____

What was locally "Babylon" in the OT becomes globally

_____

What was locally "the Euphrates River" in the OT becomes globally

_____

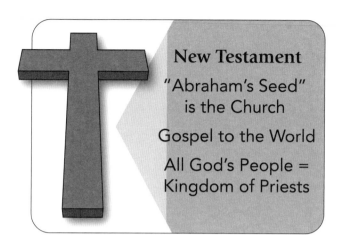

New Testament

"Abraham's Seed"
is the Church

Gospel to the World

All God's People =
Kingdom of Priests

Old Testament

Adam
Moses
Aaron
Joshua
David
Israel

New Testament

"Abraham's Seed"
is the Church

Gospel to the World

All God's People =
Kingdom of Priests

Parallel Sevens

Seven Trumpets *Revelation 8:2 – 11:18*		*Seven Bowls/Plagues* *Revelation 15:5 – 18:24*
One-third of earth burned (Rev. 8:7)	1st	Bowl poured on the earth (16:2)
One-third of sea turns to blood (Rev. 8:8-9)	2nd	Sea turns to blood (Rev. 16:3)
One-third of rivers and springs turn bitter (8:10-11)	3rd	Rivers and springs turn to blood (16:4)
One-third of sun, moon, and stars (8:12)	4th	Sun (16:10-11)
Darkness from the Abyss (9:1-2)	5th	Darkness on the beast's throne (16:10)
The great river Euphrates (9:14)	6th	The great river Euphrates (16:12)
Loud voices in heaven; "Christ will reign forever" (11:15)	7th	Loud voice from the temple throne; "It is done" (16:17)

SESSION 2

The Seven Beatitudes/Blessings in Revelation

Revelation 1:3 – "**Blessed** is the one who reads aloud the words of this prophecy, and blessed are those who hear it and take to heart what is written in it, because the time is near."

Revelation 14:13 – "Then I heard a voice from heaven say, 'Write: **Blessed** are the dead who die in the Lord from now on.' 'Yes,' says the Spirit, 'they will rest from their labor, for their deeds will follow them.'"

Revelation 16:15 – "'Look, I come like a thief! **Blessed** is the one who stays awake and remains clothed, so as not to go naked and be shamefully exposed.'"

Revelation 19:9 – "Then the angel said to me, 'Write this: "**Blessed** are those who are invited to the wedding supper of the Lamb!"' And he added, 'These are the true words of God.'"

Revelation 20:6 – "**Blessed** and holy are those who share in the first resurrection. The second death has no power over them, but they will be priests of God and of Christ and will reign with him for a thousand years."

Revelation 22:7 – "'Look, I am coming soon! **Blessed** is the one who keeps the words of the prophecy written in this scroll.'"

Revelation 22:14 – "'**Blessed** are those who wash their robes, that they may have the right to the tree of life and may go through the gates into the city.'"

[Handwritten margin notes:]
½ way through Rev before a beatitude is mentioned again. # are symbols not statics

 # 4 = whole earth
 # 12
 # 10 complete - testing 10 days dirt

7s in the Book of Revelation

The number seven (7) occurs more frequently than any other number in the Book of Revelation. Symbolically this combines God (the number three) with the world (the number four). When God is added to the world the result is completion (3 + 4 = 7). Some point to the number seven as the symbol of perfection. Paul wrote, "You are complete in Him (Christ)" (Colossians 2:10 NKJV).

Where have you found the number seven in the Book of Revelation? Some places it's obvious. Other places are not so obvious. And there are some that we would consider to be obscure. This isn't a comprehensive listing of all the sevens in Revelation, but it provides a start for the person interested in sleuthing out this important number. Add your own to these lists of seven.

Obvious

    7 Churches (Rev. 2-3)
    7 Seals (Rev. 6:1-8:1)
    7 Trumpets (Rev. 8:2-11:18)
    7 Plagues (Rev. 15:5-16:21)

Not so obvious

    7 Sections of the book (pyramid/chiastic structure)—
        see page 30
    7 Introductory sanctuary scenes—see page 132
    7 Beatitudes—see page 26
    7 Spirits before the throne (Rev. 1:4; 3:1; 4:5; 5:6)

Obscure

    7 Doxologies (Rev. 1:5-6; 4:9-10; 4:10-11; 5:12; 5:13;
        7:12; 19:1)
    7 Worship responses from heaven's angels (Rev. 7:12)
    7 Woes (Rev. 8:13; 9:12; 11:14; 12:12; 18:10: 18:16; 18:19)
    7 Uses of the word "Come/Coming" in the epilogue
        (Rev. 22:6-21)

What Does that NUMBER Mean?

Numbers in the Book of Revelation are typically symbolic, which means they represent qualities rather than quantities. Sometimes the numbers are blatant, and other times they are subtle.

3 _____

4 _____

7 (3+4) _____

6 _____

12 (3x4) _____

10 _____

1,000 (10x10x10) _____

_____

24 (12+12) _____

_____

144,000 (12x12x1,000) _____

_____

Seven Sanctuary Scenes Precede the Seven Major Divisions in Revelation

Rev. 1:9-20   Seven Churches

_____

_____

Rev. 4-5   Seven Seals

_____

_____

Rev. 8:2-5   Seven Trumpets

_____

_____

Rev. 11:19   The Heart of the Book

_____

_____

Rev. 15:5-8   Seven Last Bowls/Plagues

_____

_____

Rev. 19:1-10   Christ Conquers Sin Forever

_____

_____

Rev. 21:2-8   New Jerusalem

_____

_____

The Book of Revelation

Pyramid (Chiastic)
Structure

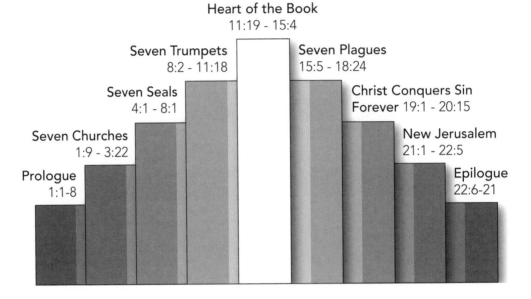

Heart of the Book
11:19 - 15:4

Seven Trumpets
8:2 - 11:18

Seven Plagues
15:5 - 18:24

Seven Seals
4:1 - 8:1

Christ Conquers Sin
Forever 19:1 - 20:15

Seven Churches
1:9 - 3:22

New Jerusalem
21:1 - 22:5

Prologue
1:1-8

Epilogue
22:6-21

The Seven Keys for Explaining Revelation

For any Book of the Bible

1. Literary context

2. Historical/Cultural context

3. Key words

4. Compare with other Scripture

For the Book of Revelation, we also add

5. Look for Old Testament roots

6. Jesus changes everything
    (Literal becomes spiritual; local becomes global)

7. Structure in the Book of Revelation
    (parallels; symbolic numbers; pyramid)

SESSION 2

The Seven Churches
Revelation 1:1-3:22

Basic Outline

Intro: Review the seven keys of interpretation by identifying key points in Revelation 1.

A. **Introductory Sanctuary Scene:** Jesus walks among the candlesticks.

B. **The Seven Churches.**

1. Introductory background for each city.

2. The message to the church there.

3. Consideration of the message for that church.

4. Promise to the victorious.

5. A personal application.

   a. Ephesus (Rev. 2:1-7).

   b. Smyrna (Rev. 2:8-11).

   c. Pergamum (Rev. 2:12-17).

   d. Thyatira (Rev. 2:18-29).

   e. Sardis (Rev. 3:1-6).

   f. Philadelphia (Rev. 3:7-13).

   g. Laodicea (Rev. 3:14-22).

C. **Summary Statement:** Immanuel (God is with us).

Which church do you identify with personally?

Who's That?
Revelation 1:12-18

- Seven golden lampstands (Exodus 25:31-37; Zechariah 4:2)

- Someone like a son of man (Daniel 7:13-14)

- Dressed in a robe reaching down to his feet
  (Exodus 28:4; 1 Samuel 18:4)

- Golden sash around his chest (Exodus 28:4)

- Hair on his head was white like wool, as white as snow
  (Daniel 7:9)

- Eyes were like blazing fire (Daniel 10:6)

- Feet like bronze glowing in a furnace (Daniel 10:6)

- Voice like the sound of rushing waters (Ezekiel 43:2)

- Seven stars in his right hand (Daniel 12:3)

- A sharp, double-edged sword coming out of his mouth
  (Isaiah 49:2; Psalm 149:6)

- Face like the sun shining in all its brilliance
  (Matthew 17:2)

- I fell at his feet as though dead
  (Joshua 5:14; Ezekiel 1:28; Daniel 8:17)

- He placed his right hand on me (Daniel 10:10)

- He said, "Do not be afraid" (Daniel 10:12; Matthew 17:7)

- I am the first and the last (Isaiah 43:10-13; 44:6)

- I am the Living One; I was dead, and now I am alive for
  ever and ever (1 Corinthians 15:20-26)

- I hold the keys of death and Hades (Revelation 20:4)

Church 1 – Ephesus
Revelation 2:1-7

Cultural Background
A significant port city where Paul started a church. There was a religious riot in which people shouted "Great is Diana/ Artemis of the Ephesians" for hours (see Acts 19:23-41). Diana (Roman)/Artemis (Greek) was the goddess of fertility and her temple in Ephesus was one of the seven wonders of the ancient world. Two other temples in the city existed for emperor worship. Paul's book of Ephesians was addressed to this church (see Ephesians 2:19-21; 5:21-32; 6:10-18). John was the pastor in Ephesus before he was exiled to Patmos.

Demetrius
Tree of assylum
Idol of Diana was
buried

How the Cultural Background Relates to This Church
Ephesus was a religiously competitive environment. The church was vigilant in fighting against the cultural onslaught on Christianity. Love is a key element, as is worship and grandeur.

The Positives
The church is vigilant, persevering, and uncompromising. They hate the practices of the Nicolaitans (who are they?—don't know but compare with the church in Pergamum (Rev. 2:14-15)—hold to the teaching of Balaam. Nicolaos and Balaam are the Greek and Hebrew equivalents of "one who destroys/ conquers the people." According to Numbers 31:16, Balaam was the instigator of idolatry and fornication among the Israelites.

The Negatives
Just one thing: missing their first love. *How important is that?*

The Need
R & R (Remember and Repent).

The Jesus Element
Holding/seizing the seven stars in his right hand (Rev. 1:12-13, 20) and walks among the seven golden lampstands (Lev. 26:11-12).

The Promise to the Victorious
Tree of Life in the Paradise of God (Garden of Eden). Return to first things—like the Garden of Eden.

Church 2 – Smyrna
Revelation 2:8-11

Cultural Background
First city in Asia to erect a temple for *Dea Roma* (the worship of Rome). This is where Christians were first accused of being atheists and disloyal to government for their refusal to worship the emperor as a god. A large Jewish synagogue in Smyrna was also hostile to Christians. *Atheies Cannabbdals*

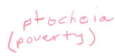
ptocheia (poverty)

How the Cultural Background Relates to This Church
This church has no allies. It is on its own—it lost the covering and respectability of being grouped with the Jews and the government is against it; hence the persecution. This church has nothing at all, except for Jesus!

The Positives
Christ knows their affliction and poverty "but you are rich." Christ knows the slander of those who say they are Jews but are of the synagogue of Satan (how would Jesus know?).

The Negatives
Nothing negative is mentioned. Would you join this church?

The Need
Hang on, you're going to be persecuted 10 days. Compare with Daniel 1:8, 12, 20 of persecution/testing…10 times testing, 10 times smarter.

Be faithful unto death, and I will give you the "crown" of life. There are two Greek words for "crown" *stephanos* (victory crown) and *diadema* (royal/kingly crown). This one is *stephanos*…the victory crown.

The Jesus Element
First and last, died and came to life again (Rev. 1:17-18).

Jesus is comprehensive, so don't be afraid of temporary trouble, and don't be afraid of death. Jesus is our role model and conquering king.

The Promise to the Victorious
The victor's crown

You will not be hurt by the second death (Rev. 20:14-15). See also Luke 12:4-5.

Church 3 – Pergamum
Revelation 2:12-17

Cultural Background
Temples erected to Zeus, Athena, Dionysus, Asclepios.

Annually burn incense to the godhead of Caesar and then you get a certificate to trade; otherwise you can be killed.

When the governor passed through the city, a person walked in front of him carrying a large, two-edged sword to signify his authority.

How the Cultural Background Relates to This Church
How can one be a Christian in Pergamum, a place with so many gods, and still survive the economic pressure and powers?

The Positives
They remain true to Christ's name. They didn't renounce their faith in Christ, even in the days of the martyr Antipas (we know nothing about this specific person). He became a martyr/witness, as Jesus did earlier.

The Negatives
Some hold to the teaching of Balaam—food sacrificed to idols and sexual immorality. See Numbers 22:21-23, 31. Angel with a sword drawn (compare with Acts 15:19-20).

The Need
Repent or Christ will come and fight against the Balaamites with the sword of his mouth (compare with Numbers 25:4-9).

The Jesus Element
The One who has the sharp, double-edged sword (Rev. 1:16).

The Promise to the Victorious
Give the hidden manna—in contrast to food sacrificed to idols.

White stone with a new name which no one knows—white is favorable judgment (in contrast to the black stone). Also given to the victor at the games, with the name in it, entitling the recipient to special honors and privileges at public festivals. A name "no one knows" represents power over a person (Rev. 19:12 – Christ comes with a name that no one knows).

[handwritten note:] started making parchment. Lots of temples. Caesar had to bow down to him. Also give him insense

[handwritten note:] Acts 10

[side tab:] SESSION 3

Church 4 – Thyatira
Revelation 2:18-29

Cultural Background
Not a major city—no emperor worship or attacks from Jews; mainly poor laborers (in contrast to Pergamum). But Christians have a problem with trade guilds and their festivals. They were expected to attend these festivals that included drunkenness and immorality.

How the Cultural Background Relates to This Church
While not experiencing the political pressures of other churches, the church is still isolated from the mainstream.

The Positives
Their love, faith, service, and perseverance are good, and they're getting better.

The Negatives
They tolerate the woman Jezebel (reference to 1 Kings 16:31-33?)—leading people to immorality and food sacrificed to idols. The problem wasn't from outside of the church but from within the congregation.

The Need
Repent and hold fast until Jesus comes.

The Jesus Element
He who searches hearts and minds—an allusion to Rev. 1:12-15 (cf. Daniel 10:6). One who is like a Son of Man, whose eyes are like blazing fire and whose feet are like burnished bronze. Jesus reads through the surface and gets to the heart (can't just go through the motions or fake it).

The Promise to the Victorious
Authority over the nations (see Psalm 2:8-9), rule with an iron scepter and dash them to pieces like pottery.

Give them the morning star (see Rev. 22:16), sure word of prophecy (2 Peter 1:19) makes it through the night.

Church 5 – Sardis
Revelation 3:1-6

Cultural Background
It's a "has been" city. Had been the capital of Lydia. It was located on a steep hill that provided a natural citadel; they became lazy in protecting it. Cyrus the Persian and Antiochus the Roman both captured the city by surprise, coming at night and finding nobody standing guard.

Patron deity was goddess Kybele. This goddess was believed to possess the power of restoring the dead to life.

How the Cultural Background Relates to This Church
The church parallels the city—a dying church—"you have a reputation that you are alive, but you are dead." Your works are not fulfilling. "Remember" and "Repent." Stay vigilant.

The Positives
A few people do not have unclean garments.

The Negatives
Your deeds are unfinished. You're asleep—wake up! You haven't kept guard.

The Need
Remember and repent. Also, "Wake up" and "Strengthen."

The Jesus Element
The One who holds the seven spirits (spirit = pneuma = breath/life) of God and the seven stars (Rev. 1:2, 16)—this is what brings you back to life—the Spirit of God. The seven stars remind them that Christ has them in his hands.

The Promise to the Victorious
Dressed in white (anticipation of Rev. 6:11; 7:14).

Name not blotted out of the Book of Life.

Jesus will acknowledge their names before the Father and his angels (Matt. 10:32; Luke 12:8-9).

Church 6 – Philadelphia
Revelation 3:7-13 *Brotherly love. Him who is holy & true*

Cultural Background
Unstable area due to earthquakes. On a plateau, functioned as the doorway of Greek culture to the those throughout Asia.
Slept in huts at night. because of earthquakes

How the Cultural Background Relates to This Church
An open door for spreading Christ (rather than Greek culture).

The Positives
Deeds are good, persevering.

Keep Christ's word.

Do not deny Christ's name.

The Negatives
You look bad, but you're actually doing fine—keep it going!

The Need
Hold what you have so no one will take your crown (*stephanos*).

Enemy Jews will come and fall at your feet.

Jesus will keep you from the hour of testing.

The Jesus Element
He holds the key of David/death and hell (Rev. 1:18 cf. with Isaiah 22:22 key of David).

The Promise to the Victorious
Will keep you from the hour of trial coming on the whole world.

You will be a pillar (a support that is fixed, not moveable) in the temple. *Never have to leave it (earthquake)*

Christ will write on them the name of God (cf. with 144,000 in Rev. 14:1), and the name of the city of God, and God's new name.

Isa 22:22
Key to storehouse of whole kingdom.

Church 7 – Laodicea *faithful & true witness*
Revelation 3:14-22

Cultural Background
Very wealthy, great commercial and banking city where gold was stored. When hit with an earthquake, they refused outside help.

Medical school known for treatment of eye diseases.

Clothing manufacturing was a fine quality of soft and glossy black wool used for garments and carpets.

Water from hot springs six miles north had an aqueduct. The water was good enough to bathe in, but was distasteful to drink and not useful for healing the sick.   *made an adequate from city 4mi E*

How the Cultural Background Relates to This Church
Replicates it! Rich and increased with goods and have need of nothing.

The Positives
Nothing positive gets mentioned.

The Negatives
You are blind, poor, naked (and you don't even know it).

The Need
Gold—faith that is tested (1 Peter 1:7).

Clothes (white raiment)—(Rev. 3:4-5; 6:11; 7:9, 13-14).

Eyesalve—to truly see (Eph. 1:17-18; Psalm 119:18; 2 Cor. 4:17-18).

Rebuke and discipline (Hebrews 12:5-11); be zealous and repent (not a matter of only remembering).

Open the door and let Jesus into your church!
Not bad people. lukewarm

The Jesus Element
The One who is the Amen (in truth; so be it) exposes.

The faithful and true witness—what is your witness?

The beginning of God's creation—everything comes from God.

The Promise to the Victorious
Only one promise—sit with Jesus on his throne. What would that include?   *Just as I overcame and sit by my father*

Song of Solomon 5:2

Promises Given to the Seven Churches

Ephesus
Eat from the Tree of Life

Smyrna
The victor's crown
Not hurt by the second death

Pergamum
Hidden manna
A white stone
A new name

Thyatira
Authority over the nations
Rule with an iron scepter
Dash others to pieces like pottery
The morning star

Sardis
Walk with Jesus
Be dressed in white
Their names will not be blotted from the Book of Life
Be acknowledged before the Father
Be acknowledged before his angels

Philadelphia
Be kept from the hour of trial coming on the whole world
Will be pillars in the temple
Will never leave the temple
Will have written on them the name of God
Will have written on them the name of the city of God
Will have written on them God's new name

Laodicea
Sit with Jesus on His throne *but had nothing*

Summary Statement 1
Revelation 1:1 – 3:22

Immanuel (God is with us)

The Seven Seals
Revelation 4:1-8:1

Basic Outline

Intro: Review the seven churches. Jesus was walking among the candlesticks.

Summary: Immanuel—"God is with us."

A. **Introductory Sanctuary Scene:**

1. The longest in the whole book.

2. Moves from earth to heaven in the first century AD.

3. Revelation 4—Throne in heaven, God the Father, 24 elders, 7 spirits, 4 living creatures. Who's missing? *Jesus*

4. Revelation 5—the Lamb, pretty obvious this is Jesus! Celebration!

(Pattern of 4-2-interlude-1 for the seven seals.)

B. **The Seven Seals.**

1. Overview of the first four seals—Revelation 6:1-8.

2. First seal—Rev. 6:1-2. White horse, bow, crown, conquering.

3. Second seal—Rev. 6:3-4. Red horse, removes peace, slays, sword.

4. Third seal—Rev. 6:5-6. Black horse, scales, famine conditions.

5. Fourth seal—Rev. 6:7-8. Pale horse, death, Hades.

6. Fifth seal—Rev. 6:9-11. Souls under the altar cry out, "How long?"

7. Sixth seal—Rev. 6:12-17. Day of the Lord; Lamb's wrath. Who can stand?

8. The 144,000—Rev. 7:1-8. Sealing/marking. Number literal or symbolic?

9. Seven clues. The same as "the great multitude" before the throne.

10. Rev. 14:1-5—The 144,000 follow the Lamb wherever he goes.

11. Seventh seal—Rev. 8:1. Silence in heaven for half an hour.

C. **Summary Statement:** Take heaven's perspective and follow the Lamb instead of the world.

Who's That Around the Throne?

24 Elders
Revelation 4:4, 10

- Dressed in white (God's faithful people— Rev. 3:4-5, 18; 6:11; 7:9, 13-14)
- Crowns of gold on their heads—*stephanos* crown of victory
- They cast their crowns before the throne in worship (Rev. 4:10)
- Worship God
- OT had 24 courses of priestly service (1 Chronicles 24:4-19)

Revelation 5:8

- Each has a harp—musical instrument used by David
- Golden bowls full of incense, which are the prayers of God's people
- The kingdom number (12) includes 12 OT tribes and 12 NT apostles

Four Living Creatures
Revelation 4:6-8

- Covered with eyes in front and in back—Ezekiel 10:12
- Ezekiel 1:4-10; Ezekiel 10:14
- Lion—noblest
- Ox—strongest
- Face like a man—wisest
- Flying eagle—swiftest
- Worship God

Revelation 5:8

- Each has a harp—musical instrument used by David
- Golden bowls full of incense, which are the prayers of God's people

Seven Spirits of God

Revelation 4:5

- Compare with Revelation 1:4 and 5:6

God the Father

Revelation 4:8-11

- Holy, holy holy is the Lord God Almighty, who was, and is, and is to come
- Worship him who sits on the throne; worship him who lives for ever and ever
- They lay their crowns before the throne
- You are worthy to receive glory and honor and power
- You created all things

Where Is Jesus?

SESSION 4

Rejoicing in Heaven

Revelation 4:8

(Group 1) The four living creatures say,

- Holy, holy, holy
- Is the Lord God Almighty
- Who was, and is, and is to come

Revelation 4:11

(Group 2) The 24 elders say,

- You are worthy, our Lord and God, to receive glory and honor and power,
- For you created all things, and by your will they were created and have their being.

Revelation 5:9-10

(Groups 1 and 2) The four living creatures plus the 24 elders sing a new song, saying,

- You are worthy to take the scroll and to open its seals,
- Because you were slain, and with your blood you purchased for God persons from every tribe and language and people and nation.
- You have made them to be a kingdom and priests to serve our God, and they will reign on the earth.

Revelation 5:12

(Group 3) Many angels, thousands upon thousands, and ten thousand times ten thousand. In a loud voice they say,

- Worthy is the Lamb, who was slain, to receive power and wealth and wisdom and strength and honor and glory and praise!

Revelation 5:13

(Groups 1, 2, 3, and 4) Every creature in heaven and on earth and under the earth, and on the sea, and all that is in them, say,

- To him who sits on the throne and to the Lamb be praise and honor and glory and power for ever and ever!

Four Horses of Revelation 6
Also the First Four Seals

Number	First	Second	Third	Fourth
Color	White	Red	Black	Pale
Actions	bow; crown; conquering	power to take peace; people kill each other; large sword	pair of scales; famine on grain; don't harm oil and wine	death and Hades; sword, famine, plague, wild animals
OT Roots	Zech. 6:3 Hab. 3:8-9 Zech. 9:13 Rev. 19:11	Zech. 6:2 Judges 7:22 Isa. 9:20-21 Psa. 119:165	Zech. 6:2 Lev. 26:26 Amos 8:11 Deut. 7:13	Zech. 6:3 Jer. 21:7-9 Ezek. 14:12-23 1 Chron. 21:12
Other	Roman generals rode white horses in triumph; *stephanos* crown, not *diadema*	Red = persecution; happened to the enemies of God's people, and a warning to God's people	Black is the absence of light; early stages of famine; still hope	Christ still holds the keys to death and Hades; consequences of a broken covenant

contract/covenant

Entire Christian Time

Gospel spreads

oil - holy spirit
grapes - wine
Blood of Jesus

¼ earth

Sword, Famine, Pestilence

Both Jeremiah and Ezekiel draw on the imagery from the covenant God made with Israel, with blessings for obedience and curses for disobedience or breaking the covenant (see Leviticus 26). The trio of "sword, famine and plague" describes a curse God sent via the Assyrians and Babylonians carried out when God's people broke the covenant. The "sword" came in the form of warfare. The "famine" came through laying siege to a city. And "plague" followed when people became sick and enfeebled in the besieged city. Sometimes "wild beasts" gets added, as when wild animals killed those who tried to escape from the besieged cities.

Here's an example from Jeremiah 24:10 (TNIV): "I will send the sword, famine and plague against them, until they are destroyed from the land that I gave to them and their ancestors."

And an example from Ezekiel 14:21 (TNIV): "For this is what the Sovereign Lord says: How much worse will it be when I send against Jerusalem my four dreadful judgments—sword and famine and wild beasts and plague—to kill its men and their animals."

Other examples can be found in Jeremiah:

14:12	34:17
21:9	38:2
27:8, 13	42:17
29, 17-18	42:22
32:24	44:13
32:26	

Similar statements can be found in Ezekiel:

5:12

5:17

6:11-12

When Does It End?

Theme	Gospels	Revelation
General signs of Christ's return	Mt. 24:3-14	Rev. 6:3-8
The time of great tribulation	Mt. 24:15-28	Rev. 6:9-11
The signs of Christ's Second Coming	Mt. 24:29-31	Rev. 6:12-17
The Gospel spreading	Mt. 24:14; Mk 13:10	Rev. 6:1-2
War	Mt. 24:6-7; Mk 13:7-8; Lk 21:9-10	Rev. 6:3-4
Famine	Mt. 24:7; Mk 13:8; Lk 21:11	Rev. 6:5-6
Pestilence	Lk 21:11	Rev. 6:7-8
Persecution	Mt. 24:9-10; Mk 13:9-13; Lk 21:12-17	Rev. 6:9-11
Heavenly signs	Mt. 24:29; Mk 13:24-25; Lk 21:25-26	Rev. 6:12-13
Tribes mourn	Mt. 24:30	Rev. 6:15-17
The Second Coming	Mt. 24:30; Mk 13:26; Lk 21:27	Rev. 6:17

John is Rev

How Long, O Lord?

The cry, "**How long?**" or "**How long, O Lord?**" has gone up for centuries. It is a cry for justice when things aren't fair. In the fifth seal of Revelation, the cry of the martyrs goes up to God with this question. We have all made that same cry ourselves. In has Old Testament roots, as noted below.

Revelation 6:9-10
When he opened the fifth seal, I saw under the altar the souls of those who had been slain because of the word of God and the testimony they had maintained. They called out in a loud voice, "**How long, Sovereign Lord**, holy and true, until you judge the inhabitants of the earth and avenge our blood?"

Psalm 13:1-2
How long, Lord? Will you forget me forever? **How long** will you hide your face from me? **How long** must I wrestle with my thoughts and day after day have sorrow in my heart? **How long** will my enemy triumph over me? (Additional psalms that ask "How long?" include Psalm 6:3; 35:17; 74:9-10; 79:5; 80:4; 82:2; 89:46; and 90:13.)

Habakkuk 1:2-3, 13
How long, Lord, must I call for help, but you do not listen? Why do you make me look at injustice? Why do you tolerate wrongdoing? Why are you silent while the wicked swallow up those more righteous than themselves?

Daniel 8:13-14
Then I heard a holy one speaking, and another holy one said to him, "**How long** will it take for the vision to be fulfilled—the vision concerning the daily sacrifice, the rebellion that causes desolation, the surrender of the sanctuary and the trampling underfoot of the LORD's people?" He said to me, "It will take 2,300 evenings and mornings; then the sanctuary will be reconsecrated."

This cry/prayer will be answered with justice and judgment by God, in God's time. Until then, we will continue to join with the martyrs when injustice occurs and will cry out, "How long, O Lord?"

Sealing of the 144,000

Rev 7: , 14 only places 144,000

Exodus 12:21-23
Then Moses summoned all the elders of Israel and said to them, "Go at once and select the animals for your families and slaughter the Passover lamb. Take a bunch of hyssop, dip it into the blood in the basin and put some of the blood on the top and on both sides of the doorframe. None of you shall go out of the door of your house until morning. When the LORD goes through the land to strike down the Egyptians, he will see the blood on the top and sides of the doorframe and will pass over that doorway, and he will not permit the destroyer to enter your houses and strike you down."

Ezekiel 9:4
Go throughout the city of Jerusalem and put a mark on the foreheads of those who grieve and lament over all the detestable things that are done in it.

2 Corinthians 1:21-22
Now it is God who makes both us and you stand firm in Christ. He anointed us, set his seal of ownership on us, and put his Spirit in our hearts as a deposit, guaranteeing what is to come.

Ephesians 1:13-14
And you also were included in Christ, when you heard the message of truth, the gospel of your salvation. When you believed, you were marked in him with a seal, the promised Holy Spirit, who is a deposit guaranteeing our inheritance until the redemption of those who are God's possession—to the praise of his glory.

Ephesians 4:30
And do not grieve the Holy Spirit of God, with whom you were sealed for the day of redemption. *fruit of the spirit*

2 Timothy 2:19
God's solid foundation stands firm, sealed with this inscription, "The Lord knows those who are his," and "Everyone who confesses the name of the Lord must turn away from wickedness."

Revelation is symbolic

Seals Five and Six in Revelation 6

Number	Fifth	Sixth
Scene	Souls under the altar	Great earthquake
		Sun turned black
		Moon turned blood red
		Stars fell to the earth
		Sky receded like a scroll
		Every mountain & island removed
Actions	<u>Cry out, "How long?"</u>	Kings, et al., slave and free
	Judge and avenge	call for the rocks to fall on them
	our blood	Wrath of the Lamb
	White robes given	Who can withstand it?
	Wait a little longer	Others will also be killed
OT Roots	Gen. 4:10	Ezekiel 38:19-20
	Psalm 79:1-10	Joel 2:10-11, 31
	Daniel 8:1	Isaiah 13:10; 34:4
	Rev. 3:4-5;	Matthew 24:29
	Rev. 7:9	Jeremiah 4:24
		Isaiah 2:19-21
		Nahum 1:6-7

Ps.   Come to prayer

SESSION 4

Name Those 12 Tribes

The 12 tribes in the order they are listed in these passages:

Revelation 7	*Genesis 49*	*Numbers 1:5-15*	*Ezekiel 48*
1. Judah	Reuben	Reuben	Dan
2. Reuben	Simeon	Simeon	Asher
3. Gad	Levi	Judah	Naphtali
4. Asher	Judah	Issachar	Manasseh
5. Naphtali	Zebulun	Zebulun	Ephraim
6. Manasseh	Issachar	Ephraim	Reuben
7. Simeon	Dan	Manasseh	Judah
8. Levi	Gad	Benjamin	Benjamin
9. Issachar	Asher	Dan	Simeon
10. Zebulun	Naphatali	Asher	Issachar
11. Joseph	Joseph	Gad	Zebulun
12. Benjamin	Benjamin	Naphtali	Gad

Matching the 12 tribes in these passages:

Revelation 7	*Genesis 49*	*Numbers 1:5-15*	*Ezekiel 48*
1. Reuben	Reuben	Reuben	Reuben
2. Simeon	Simeon	Simeon	Simeon
3. Judah	Judah	Judah	Judah
4. Issachar	Issachar	Issachar	Issachar
5. Zebulun	Zebulun	Zebulun	Zebulun
6. Naphtali	Naphtali	Naphtali	Naphtali
7. Gad	Gad	Gad	Gad
8. Asher	Asher	Asher	Asher
9. Benjamin	Benjamin	Benjamin	Benjamin
10. Joseph	Joseph	Ephraim	Ephraim
11. Manasseh	Levi	Manasseh	Manasseh
12. Levi	Dan	Dan	Dan

"Hearing" and "Seeing"

Revelation 1:10-13—Heard **a voice like a trumpet BUT** *saw* **someone like a son of man.**

I heard behind me a loud voice like a trumpet (vs. 10)…I turned around to see the voice that was speaking to me. And when I turned I saw seven golden lampstands, and among the lampstands was someone like a son of man (vs. 12-13).

*Revelation 5:5-6—***One of the elders** *said,* **"See the Lion of the tribe of Judah, the Root of David" BUT I** *saw* **a Lamb.**

Then one of the elders said to me, "Do not weep! See, the Lion of the tribe of Judah, the Root of David, has triumphed. He is able to open the scroll and its seven seals." Then I saw a Lamb, looking as if it had been slain, standing at the center of the throne, encircled by the four living creatures and the elders.

*Revelation 17:1-3—***One of the angels** *said,* **"I will show you the great prostitute who sits by many waters." BUT I** *saw* **a woman sitting on a scarlet beast.**

One of the seven angels who had the seven bowls came and said to me, "Come, I will show you the punishment of the great prostitute, who sits by many waters…. There I saw a woman sitting on a scarlet beast that was covered with blasphemous names and had seven heads and ten horns.

Revelation 21:9-10—One of the angels *said* to me, "I will show you the bride, the wife of the Lamb." BUT He *showed* me the Holy City, Jerusalem.

One of the seven angels who had the seven bowls full of the seven last plagues came and said to me, "Come, I will show you the bride, the wife of the Lamb." And he carried me away in the Spirit to a mountain great and high, and showed me the Holy City, Jerusalem, coming down out of heaven from God.

Revelation 7:4, 9—I *heard* the number of those who were sealed: 144,000 from all the tribes of Isreal (vs. 4). BUT I *looked*, and there was a great multitude that no one could count.

Then I heard the number of those who were sealed: 144,000 from all the tribes of Israel (vs. 4)…After this I looked, and there before me was a great multitude that no one could count, from every nation, tribe, people and language, standing before the throne and before the Lamb. They were wearing white robes and were holding palm branches in their hands (vs. 9).

SESSION 4

Summary Statement 2
Revelation 4:1-8:1

Take Heaven's perspective and follow the Lamb
instead of the world.

The Seven Trumpets *calling us to Repentance*
Revelation 8:2-11:18

Basic Outline

Intro: Review the seven seals, 144,000/great multitude.

A. The seven trumpets. Difficult! Pattern of 4-2-Interlude-1.

B. **Introductory Sanctuary Scene:** Revelation 8:2-6.
   Call to daily prayer.

C. Trumpets—OT roots.

D. **The Seven Trumpets.**

1. Trumpet 1: Revelation 8:7. God starts his warning and punishment with those who claim to be his followers; will they turn to him before he returns?

2. Trumpet 2: Revelation 8:8-9. God warns and punishes those opposed to his people so they will turn to him before he returns.

3. Trumpet 3: Revelation 8:10-11. God warns that what is supposed to give life will bring death when tainted by apostasy.

4. Trumpet 4: Revelation 8:12. The light of God gets obscured as people live without any sense or need of God.

Eagle or Vulger
5. Trumpet 5: Revelation 9:1-12. When God gives Satan the freedom to roam the earth, Satan destroys it; God wants people to pray and repent.

6. Trumpet 6: Revelation 9:13–21. When God stops protecting the wicked, they refuse to repent even though Satan intensifies his destruction of them.

(Interlude: The little scroll and the two witnesses.)

7. Trumpet 7: Revelation 11:15-18.
   The Second Coming! Woe?

8. Revelation 11:18 outlines the second half of Revelation.

E. **Summary Statement:** God warns of the need to repent; He sends and allows difficulty, destruction, and death to get people's attention; In such uncertain chaos, prayer continues to be our lifeline to God.

Trumpets in the Old Testament

War	Coronation	Call to Gather	Warning	Worship
Numbers 31:6	2 Samuel 15:10	Numbers 10:2-7	Jeremiah 4:5	Leviticus 23:24
Joshua 6:4	1 Kings 1:34, 39	Numbers 29:1	Jer. 4:19-21	1 Chronicles 15:24
Joshua 6:20	2 Kings 9:13	1 Samuel 13:3-4	Jer. 6:1-17	1 Chronicles 16:6
Judges 7:20-22	2 Kings 11:14	Nehemiah 4:20	Ezekiel 33:3-6	2 Chronicles 5:12-13
2 Chronicles 13:12		Joel 2:15-16	Amos 3:6	2 Chronicles 7:6
Job 39:25				2 Chronicles 15:14
				Ezra 3:10
				Nehemiah 12:41
				Psalm 98:4-6

Day of the Lord—Isaiah 27:13; Joel 2:1; Zephaniah 1:16; Zechariah 9:14

10:8-10

SESSION 5

Parallels Between the Seven Seals and the Seven Trumpets

Seven Seals	*Seven Trumpets*
First Seal—White horse	
Second Seal—Red horse	First Trumpet—Fire and blood Second Trumpet—Fire and blood
Third Seal—Black horse, famine	Third Trumpet—Lack of water Fourth Trumpet—Darkness
Fourth Seal—Pale horse, death	Fifth Trumpet—Destroyer
Fifth Seal—Voices at the altar Incomplete number of the saved	Sixth Trumpet—Voice at the altar Incomplete number of the murdered
Sixth Seal—The day of wrath has come	Seventh Trumpet—Your wrath has come
Seventh Seal—Silence in heaven	

Parallels Between the Seven Trumpets and the Seven Plagues/Bowls   *still warning*

	Seven Trumpets			*Seven Plagues*
First	Rev. 8:7	Earth		Rev. 16:2
Second	Rev. 8:8	Sea turns to blood		Rev. 16:3
Third	Rev. 8:10	Rivers and fountains		Rev. 16:4
Fourth	Rev. 8:12	Sun, moon, stars; sun		Rev. 16:8-9
Fifth	Rev. 9:1-11	Darkness		Rev. 16:10-11
Sixth	Rev. 9:14-21	River Euphrates		Rev. 16:12-16
Seven	Rev. 11:15	Loud voices—Kingdom has come; "It is done"		Rev. 16:17-21

10 Plagues on Egypt
Exodus 7-12

1.	Water turned to blood	Exodus 7:14-24
2.	Frogs	Exodus 8:1-15
3.	Gnats	Exodus 8:16-19
4.	Flies	Exodus 8:20-32
5.	Livestock	Exodus 9:1-7
6.	Boils	Exodus 9:8-12
7.	Hail	Exodus 9:13-35
8.	Locusts	Exodus 10:1-20
9.	Darkness	Exodus 10:21-29
10.	Death of firstborn	Exodus 11:1-10; 12:29-36

to Ezekial (handwritten)

"Inhabitants of the Earth"
(Some translations have "Those who dwell on the earth")

Revelation 6:10
They called out in a loud voice, "How long, Sovereign Lord, holy and true, until you judge the inhabitants of the earth and avenge our blood?"

Revelation 8:13
As I watched, I heard an eagle that was flying in midair call out in a loud voice: "Woe! Woe! Woe to the inhabitants of the earth, because of the trumpet blasts about to be sounded by the other three angels!"

Revelation 11:10
The inhabitants of the earth will gloat over them and will celebrate by sending each other gifts, because these two prophets had tormented those who live on the earth.

Revelation 13:8
All inhabitants of the earth will worship the beast—all whose names have not been written in the Lamb's book of life, the Lamb who was slain from the creation of the world.

Revelation 13:14
Because of the signs it was given power to perform on behalf of the first beast, it deceived the inhabitants of the earth. It ordered them to set up an image in honor of the beast who was wounded by the sword and yet lived.

Revelation 17:2
With her the kings of the earth committed adultery, and the inhabitants of the earth were intoxicated with the wine of her adulteries.

The Seven Trumpets

Notes:

9: 5th Angel given key. Given to Satan he wants to kill me but God can still save me. Better repents light goes out. 5 mos - lifespan of locust Joel talks about horses woman hair (Dan 15)

6th angel will kill 1/3 people. Still worshipped idols. Euphrates river relieved people.

Mystery of the Kingdom

Mark 4:11

He told them, "The secret [mystery] of the kingdom of God has been given to you. But to those on the outside everything is said in parables."

Romans 11:25

I do not want you to be ignorant of this mystery, brothers and sisters, so that you may not be conceited: Israel has experienced a hardening in part until the full number of the Gentiles has come in.

Romans 16:25

Now to him who is able to establish you in accordance with my gospel, the message I proclaim about Jesus Christ, in keeping with the revelation of the mystery hidden for long ages past, but now revealed and made known through the prophetic writings by the command of the eternal God, so that all the Gentiles might come to the obedience that comes from faith.

Ephesians 3:4-6

In reading this, then, you will be able to understand my insight into the mystery of Christ, which was not made known to people in other generations as it has now been revealed by the Spirit to God's holy apostles and prophets. This mystery is that through the gospel the Gentiles are heirs together with Israel, members together of one body, and sharers together in the promise in Christ Jesus.

Ephesians 3:8-10

Although I am less than the least of all the Lord's people, this grace was given to me to preach to the Gentiles the boundless riches of Christ, and to make plain to everyone the administration of this mystery, which for ages past was kept hidden in God, who created all things. His intent was that now, through the church, the manifold wisdom of God should be made known to the rulers and authorities in the heavenly realms.

1 Corinthians 15:51-52
Listen, I tell you a mystery. We will not all sleep, but we will all be changed—in a flash, in the twinkling of an eye, at the last trumpet. For the trumpet will sound, the dead will be raised imperishable, and we will be changed.

1 Timothy 3:16
Beyond all question, the mystery from which true godliness springs is great: He appeared in the flesh, was vindicated by the Spirit, was seen by angels, was preached among the nations, was believed on in the world, was taken up in glory.

Colossians 2:2-3
My goal is that they may be encouraged in heart and united in love, so that they may have the full riches of complete understanding, in order that they may know the mystery of God, namely, Christ, in whom are hidden all the treasures of wisdom and knowledge.

Colossians 1:26-27
The mystery that has been kept hidden for ages and generations, but is now disclosed to the Lord's people. To them God has chosen to make known among the Gentiles the glorious riches of this mystery, which is Christ in you, the hope of glory.

SESSION 5

Summary of the Seven Trumpets

First Trumpet

God starts his warning and punishment with those who claim to be his followers so they will truly turn to him before he returns.

Second Trumpet

God warns and punishes those opposed to his people so they will turn to him before he returns.

Third Trumpet

God warns that what is supposed to give life will bring death when tainted by apostasy.

Fourth Trumpet

The light of God gets obscured as people live without any sense or need of God.

Fifth Trumpet

When God gives Satan the freedom to roam the earth, Satan destroys it while God wants the people to pray and repent.

Sixth Trumpet

When God stops protecting the wicked, they refuse to repent even though Satan intensifies his destruction of them.

Seventh Trumpet

It all culminates with this world becoming the kingdom of God.

8th trumpet still calling them back

Revelation 11:18 Outlines the Second Half of Revelation

The nations were angry

Satan works through a sea beast and a land beast to war against God and God's people, while God and his people provide a final Gospel appeal

Your wrath has come

The seven last plagues and judgments fall on Babylon as God's wrath against those who have oppressed God's people

The time has come for judging the dead

The timing and rewards/punishments

> *Give the reward to your saints*
> God's people rewarded with a new earth and a new Jerusalem

> *Destroy the destroyers of the earth*
> The destruction of those who destroyed the earth, plus final judgment after the millennium

SESSION 5

Summary Statement 3

Revelation 8:2-11:18

- God warns of the need to repent.

- He sends and allows difficulty, destruction, and death to get people's attention.

- In such uncertain chaos, prayer continues to be our lifeline to God.

SESSION 5

The Heart of the Book – Part 1
Revelation 11:19-13:18

Basic Outline

Intro: Introductory Sanctuary Scenes to this point.

A. **Introductory Sanctuary Scene:** The Ark of the Covenant.

B. **The Woman and the Dragon**—Revelation 12:1-17.

    1. War in heaven; 2 major characters.

    2. Who's in charge of earth? Christ's activities vs. Satan's activities.

    3. War in heaven (Revelation 12:7): Michael vs. the Accuser.

    4. Time span of three and a half times, 42 months, 1,260 days.

C. **Duo-directional Verse**—Revelation 12:17. Two characteristics of God's people.

    1. Keep God's commands.

    2. Hold fast their testimony about Jesus.

D. **The Sea Beast**—Revelation 13:1-10.

    1. Looks remarkably like the dragon: 10 horns, 7 heads, 10 crowns.

    2. Sea Beast mimics Jesus; Dragon mimics God the Father.

E. **The Earth Beast**—Revelation 13:11-18.

    1. Exercises all of the authority of the first beast. Imitates the Holy Spirit.

    2. Economic coercion—political and religious collusion.

    3. Beasts and schools of interpretation.

    4. The "mark of the beast"—666.

F. **Heart of the Book of Revelation:** I will be their God; they will be my people.

    1. A false trinity seeks to swallow God's people (power & deception).

    2. God has a place for us: now plus then.

The Sanctuary in the Wilderness

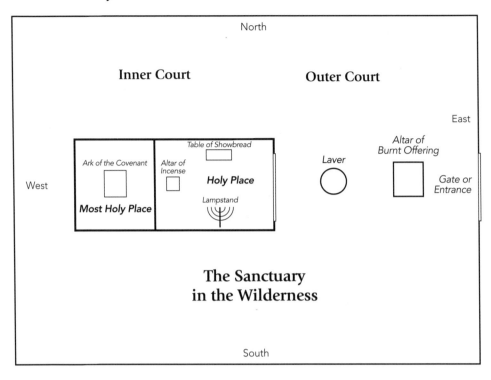

The Sanctuary
in the Wilderness

SESSION 6

The Great Conflict Between Christ and Satan During Christ's Ministry on Earth

Christ's Activities	*Satan's Activities*
CLAIM TERRITORY THROUGH	ATTACK JESUS THROUGH
1. Presence	A. Natural world
2. Overcoming disease, death, demons	B. Death, destruction
3. Blessing, redeeming	C. Direct attacks
4. Revising religion	D. Religious leaders
5. Deputizing others to spread his kingdom	E. Political and military powers

SESSION 6

Michael

The name "**Michael**" occurs only five times in the Bible. The name actually means "**Who is like God.**" Some think this refers to Jesus Christ in the role of a mighty warrior. Others think it may refer to an archangel based on a listing in the Apocrypha with other archangels. Here are the passages:

Daniel 10:13
But the prince of the Persian kingdom resisted me twenty-one days. Then **Michael**, one of the chief princes, came to help me, because I was detained there with the king of Persia.

Daniel 10:21
No one supports me against them except **Michael**, your prince.

Daniel 12:1
At that time **Michael**, the great prince who protects your people, will arise. There will be a time of distress such as has not happened from the beginning of nations until then. But at that time your people—everyone whose name is found written in the book—will be delivered.

Jude 1:9
But even the archangel **Michael**, when he was disputing with the devil about the body of Moses, did not himself dare to condemn him for slander but said, "The Lord rebuke you!"

Enoch 53:6 (apocryphal book)
States that **Michael**, along with Gabriel, Raphael and Phanuel, all archangels, will be strengthened during the Battle of Armageddon.

Revelation 12:7-8
Then war broke out in heaven. **Michael** and his angels fought against the dragon, and the dragon and his angels fought back. But he was not strong enough, and they lost their place in heaven.

Time Lines

1260 Days = 42 Months = 3 ½ Years

Rev. 11:3	Rev. 11:2	Rev. 12:14
Rev. 12:6	Rev. 13:5	Rev. 13:5
		Dan. 7:25
		Dan. 12:7

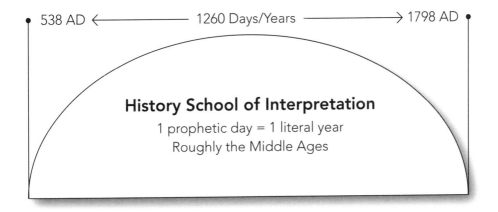

538 AD ⟵——— 1260 Days/Years ———→ 1798 AD

History School of Interpretation
1 prophetic day = 1 literal year
Roughly the Middle Ages

Questions for You

Revelation 12:17 is a "duo-directional" verse. It summarizes the previous verses and points forward to the next verses.

> **"Then the dragon was enraged at the woman**
> **and went off to wage war against**
> **the rest of her offspring—**
> **those who keep God's commands and**
> **hold fast their testimony about Jesus."**

Questions

Question 1:
Where have you seen the dragon's rage?

_____

_____

Question 2:
What are God's commands?

Love & obey, 10 commandment

_____

Question 3:
Which of God's commands do you follow and which ones do you ignore or put at a lower level?

_____

_____

Question 4:
Where have you found the testimony about Jesus?

_____

_____

Question 5:
What is your testimony about Jesus?

Rev 10:   Rev 1:

_____

_____

SESSION 6

True Trinity and False Trinity – 1

God the Father	*The Dragon/Satan*
God's dwelling place is in heaven (Rev. 4-5)	His place is in heaven (Rev. 12:3, 7-8)
He has a throne (Rev. 4-5; 7:9-15; 19:4)	He has a throne (Rev. 13:2; 2:13)
Gives power, throne, authority to Christ (Matt. 28:18; Rev. 2:27; 3:21; Rev. 4-5)	Gives power, throne, authority to sea beast (Rev. 13:2,4)
He is worshiped (Rev. 4:10; 15:4)	He is worshiped (Rev. 13:4)
He lives and reigns forever (Rev. 4:9; 5:13; 11:15)	He is destroyed forever (Rev. 20:9-10)

Adapted from Ranko Stefanovic's *Revelation of Jesus Christ.*

True Trinity and False Trinity – 2

Jesus Christ	*The Sea Beast*
Comes from water to begin ministry (Luke 3:21-23)	Comes from water to begin his activity (Rev. 13:1)
Seeing me is seeing the Father (John 14:9)	Resembles the dragon (Rev. 12:3; 13:1)
Has many *diadema* crowns (Rev. 19:12)	Has 10 *diadema* crowns (Rev. 13:1)
The Lamb with seven horns (Rev. 5:6)	Has 10 horns on his head (Rev. 13:1)
Receives power, throne, authority from the Father (Mt. 28:18; Rev. 2:27; 4-5)	Receives power, throne, authority from the dragon (13:2, 4)
3½ years ministry (Gospel of John)	42 months of activity (Rev. 13:5)
He was slain (Rev. 5:6)	He was slain (Rev. 13:3)
Resurrected (Rev. 1:18)	Came back to life (Rev. 13:3)
Received worship after resurrection (Mt. 28:17)	Received worship after mortal wound healed (Rev. 13:3-4, 8)
All authority in heaven and earth given after the Resurrection (Mt. 28:18)	Given universal authority over the earth after mortal wound healed (Rev. 13:7)
Michael = Who is like God (Rev. 12:7)	Who is like the beast? (Rev. 13:4)
Targets the whole world (Rev. 5:9; 10:11; 14:6)	Targets the whole world (Rev. 13:7; 17:15)

Adapted from Ranko Stefanovic's *Revelation of Jesus Christ.*

SESSION 6

True Trinity and False Trinity – 3

The Holy Spirit	*The Earth Beast*
Called the Spirit of truth, guides people to salvation (John 16:13; Rev. 22:17)	Called the false prophet, deceives people (Rev. 16:13; 19:20; 20:10)
Christ-like (John 14:26; 16:14)	Lamb-like (Rev. 13:11)
Exercises all the authority of Christ (John 16:13-14)	Exercises all the authority of the sea beast (Rev. 13:12)
Directs worship to Christ (Acts 5:29-32)	Directs worship to sea beast (Rev. 13:12, 15)
Performs great signs (Acts 4:30-31)	Performs great signs (Rev. 13:13; 19:20)
Comes in fire at Pentecost (Acts 2)	Brings fire down from heaven (Rev. 13:13)
Gives life/breath of life (Rom. 8:11)	Gives life/breath to the beast's image (Rev. 13:15)
Applies the seal on the forehead (2 Cor. 1:22; Eph. 1:13; 4:30)	Applies the mark on the hand or forehead (Rev. 13:16)

Adapted from Ranko Stefanovic's *Revelation of Jesus Christ.*

SESSION 6

Images in Scripture

Revelation 13:14-17
Earth beast orders the inhabitants of the earth to set up an image in honor of the sea beast.

Daniel 3
King Nebuchadnezzar creates an image that contrasts with the image in his dream (Daniel 2) and summons everyone to come and worship the image on the threat of death.

Exodus 32
The Israelites worship an image/golden calf acclaimed as the gods who brought Israel out of Egypt (vs. 4). False worshipers might be blotted out of God's book (vs. 33). God sends a plague because they worshiped the image (vs. 35).

1 Kings 12
Jeroboam, the new king of the 10 Northern tribes of Israel, feared people would still go to Jerusalem to worship Yahweh. So he created two golden calves and set one up in Dan and the other in Bethel. He said, "Here are your gods, Israel, who brought you up out of Egypt" (verse 28). A prophet from Judah denounced him (1 Kings 13). After that, every king of Israel considered evil gets labeled as one who followed the sins of Jeroboam.

Genesis 1:26-27
Humans are made in God's image. We have been trying to return the favor—trying to make God in our image—ever since the Fall.

You're a Beast!

Different Schools of Interpretation have their own views of the two beasts presented in Revelation 13. Here are the general views of the four schools.

School of Interpretation	*Sea Beast*	*Land Beast*
Past (Preterist)	Roman Empire, Emperor Nero	Paganism, emperor cult, Governor of Judea Jewish religious system
Future (Futurist)	Revived Roman Empire	Antichrist, Pope or False Jewish Messiah
History (Historicist)	Roman Empire	Roman Catholic Church
Adventist version	Roman Catholic Church	United States
Spiritual (Idealist/Symbolic)	Political/Social evil	False religion, False philosophy

SESSION 6

666

Vicarius Filii Dei

Latin for Vicar of the Son of God, the pope's title on the hat worn for the pope's coronations until the 17th century.

V = 5	F = 0	D = 500
I = 1	I = 1	E = 0
C = 100	L = 50	I = 1
A = 0	I = 1	
R = 0	I = 1	
I = 1		
U/V = 5		
S = 0		TOTAL = 666

NRWN QSR

"Neron Kaiser" which is the Hebrew for Caesar Nero. Based on the value of Hebrew letters:

N = 50	Q = 100	
R = 200	S = 60	
W = 6	R = 200	
N = 50		TOTAL = 666

Beast

The word "beast" occurs 36 times in the book of Revelation.
Add up 1-36 (1+2+3+4+... 35+36) = 666.

Ellen Gould White

A significant person in the starting of the Seventh-day Adventist Church; a person Adventists believe has the spiritual gift of prophecy (messages from God).

E = 0	G = 0	W/V+V = 10	
L = 50	O = 0	H = 0	
L = 50	U/V = 5	I - 1	
E = 0	L = 50	T = 0	
N = 0	D = 500	E = 0	TOTAL = 666

Ronald Wilson Reagan

The 40th president of the United States (1981-1989). Add the numbers of letters in his name:

Ronald = 6	
Wilson = 6	
Reagan = 6	TOTAL = 666

Revelation 13 and Daniel 3

Topic	Revelation 13	Daniel 3
Image	verse 14	verse 1
Worship the image	verse 15	verse 5
Death threat for not worshiping the image	verse 15	verse 6
Universality	verse 16	verse 2
Number "6" associated with the image	verse 18	verse 1

- Daniel 3 will be repeated on a global scale toward the end of the world.

- The final crisis will be one of worship.

- Those who worship God will appear to lose, but will miraculously be delivered by God.

The Heart of the Book – Part 2
Revelation 14:1-15:4

Basic Outline

Intro: Review the introductory sanctuary scene, the false trinity and the woman who represents God's people.

This session reveals God's response to the false trinity by presenting the Lamb, the 144,000, messages from three angels, and more.

A. **God's Response to the False Trinity**—Revelation 14:1-13.

    1. Review Revelation 14:1-5; The Lamb and the 144,000.

    2. Simplified version of the 3 Angels' Messages

    3. First Angel's Message—Revelation 14:6-7.

    4. Second Angel's Message—Revelation 14:8.

    5. Third Angel's Message—Revelation 14:9-13.

    6. After the 3 Angels' Messages—Revelation 14:12. Patience, Keep God's commands, faithful to Jesus.

B. **Two Harvests**—Revelation 14:14-20.

    1. Three more angels.

    2. Two harvest seasons in Israel—grain in the Spring; grapes in the Fall.

    3. Praise God with singing!—Song of Moses and the Lamb.

C. **Summary Statement:** Look to God. Will you worship the True Trinity or the false trinity?

Characteristics of the 144,000
As found in Revelation 14:1-5

Question: Are these literal or symbolic?

- Stand with the Lamb

- On Mount Zion

- Name of the Lamb on their foreheads

- Name of God the Father on their foreheads

- Sing a new song

- Before the throne, four living creatures and the elders

- Are redeemed from the earth

- Did not defile themselves with women

- Remained virgins

- Follow the Lamb wherever he goes

- Purchased among the human race

- Offered as firstfruits to God and the Lamb

- No lie in their mouths

- Are blameless

Three Angels' Messages of Rev. 14

The Simplified Version

First Angel's Message (Revelation 14:6-7)

- Proclaim the eternal Gospel to the whole world   *Not a new gospel Worship Him.*
   Fear God   Give him glory, hour of His justice is come.
- Turn to God   *worship Creator.*

- Judgment now

- Worship the Creator   *Big than I am*

Second Angel's Message (Revelation 14:8)

- Satan's kingdom loses   *Gen 10 & 11   Isa*

Third Angel's Message (Revelation 14:9-12)   *Wrath of God's response to adultry*

- Satan's kingdom loses badly and won't return   *says Stop.*

- God's people need patience as they trust Jesus

How Many Angels Do You See?

Seventh-day Adventists notice three angels in Revelation 14 that most other religious groups pass over without much notice. Are there other angels in Revelation 14 that people miss?

First Three Angels of Rev. 14	One Like a Son of Man	Last Three Angels of Rev. 14
"I saw another angel" "he said with a loud voice" the hour of God's judgment has come. (vs. 6-7)	On a white cloud, with a golden crown, and a sickle ready to reap. (vs. 14)	"Another angel came out of the temple, calling with a loud voice." "The hour to reap has come." (vs. 15)
"Another angel, a second, followed. Babylon loses; she makes other drink the wine of her sexual immorality. (vs. 8)		"Another angel came out of the temple in heaven" (vs. 17) He also had a sharp sickle; told to harvest the grapes and put them into the winepress of God's wrath.
"Another angel, a third, followed, saying with a loud voice." (vs. 9) Those who worship something other than God, drink the wine of God's wrath, and will suffer by fire.		"Another angel came out from the altar." "Called with a loud voice." (vs. 18) Has authority over fire.

Whom Do You Fear?

"Fear" means both being scared and having reverence. In Revelation 14:7 "Fear God" means taking God seriously. Here are some Old Testament roots for the word "fear."

Fear: a relationship of full surrender to God and His will

1 Samuel 12:14, 24	Psalm 40:3
2 Chronicles 6:31	Jeremiah 32:39
Nehemiah 7:2	Jeremiah 44:10
Job 1:9	Haggai 1:12

Fear: overwhelmed to the point of belief

Exodus 14:31

Fear: characteristic of God's servants

Genesis 22:12	Psalm 22:23
1 Kings 18:3	Psalm 33:18
1 Kings 12:2	Malachi 3:16
2 Kings 4:1	Malachi 4:2

Fear: the starting point for wisdom

Psalm 111:10

Proverbs 1:7

Proverbs 9:10

Fear: response of doing what is right

Exodus 18:21

Leviticus 19:14, 32

Leviticus 25:17, 36, 43

Fear: avoiding evil

Job 1:1, 8

Proverbs 3:7

Proverbs 16:6

How Long Is "Forever?"

Fire and sulfur with smoke ascending "for ever and ever" (Rev. 14:10-11; see also Rev. 19:3 and Rev. 20:10). These have Old Testament roots.

Genesis 19:24, 28
God rains fire and sulfur on Sodom and Gomorrah. Abraham sees smoke ascending from the earth. According to Jude 1:7 these two cities experience the punishment of eternal fire.

Isaiah 34:8-10
God will punish Edom with fire and sulfur, with blazing pitch. It won't be quenched night or day; its smoke will rise forever. From generation to generation it will lie desolate.

The purpose of fire is to consume, never to preserve. Sodom and Gomorrah are no longer burning. Neither is Edom. They burned until they were completely consumed, never to return.

The contrast can be seen in the most famous verse of the Bible—**John 3:16** – "For God so loved the world that He gave his only begotten Son, that whosoever believes in Him *will not perish but have everlasting life.*" A person who burns literally for ever and ever still has eternal life (even though it would be a miserable eternal life). But according to John 3:16, only believers in Jesus have everlasting life. All others "perish." The *punishment* is eternal; the *punishing* is not eternal.

"Smoke and sulfur ascending for ever and ever" means total and complete consumption, never to return.

False Trinity Countered by the Three Angels' Messages

False Trinity *(Rev. 12 and 13)*	*Three Angels' Messages* *(Rev. 14)*
Dragon	**First Angel's Message**
Terror on the earth and sea	Good news (Gospel) to the whole earth
The devil has come with great anger	Fear God and give Him glory
Accuser of the brethren	Hour of judgment has come
War against those who follow Jesus	Worship the Creator
Sea Beast	**Second Angel's Message**
Overcomes God's holy people	Babylon loses
Those on the earth follow in awe	Fall of "Babylon the Great"
Authority to rule the world	Babylon guilty of worldwide immorality
Earth Beast	**Third Angel's Message**
Requires all to worship the sea beast	Don't worship the beast and its image
Does miracles; deceives the world	Patiently trust Jesus
Orders an image made to the beast	No rest for the wicked
Gives life to the image	Smoke/Destruction rises forever
Death decree if you don't worship	God's wrath for beast worshipers
Economic coercion— mark of the beast	Doom for those who accept the mark

SESSION 7

Where Can I Find That Song?

The "song of Moses and the song of the Lamb" found in Revelation 15:3-4 is composed of several Old Testament roots.

Great and marvelous are your works
Psalm 111:2-3

Righteous and true are your ways
Deuteronomy 32:4; Psalm 145:17

King of the nations
Jeremiah 10:6-7

Who will not fear you, O Lord, and glorify your name?
Jeremiah 10:7

For you only are holy
1 Samuel 2:2

All the nations will come and worship before you
Psalm 86:9, Jeremiah 16:19

Sing This Song!

Group 1	*Group 2*
Great and marvelous are your deeds, Lord God Almighty.	
	Just and true are your ways, King of the nations.
Who will not fear you, Lord, and bring glory to your name?	
	For you alone are holy.
All nations will come and worship before you	
	For your righteous acts have been revealed.

SESSION 7

Summary Statement 4
Revelation 11:19-15:4

- Look to God.

- Will you worship the True Trinity or the false trinity?

- Worship of the True Trinity requires an enduring trust in Jesus.

The Seven Bowls/Plagues

Revelation 15:5-18:24 *literal or sybolic?*

Basic Outline

Intro: Review the heart of the book from the previous two sessions.
Covenant: "I will by your God and you will be my people.

A. **Introductory Sanctuary Scene:** Revelation 15:5-8—
same as the previous one? No, tabernacle of the
"testimony" rather than "covenant."

B. **The 7 Plagues**—Revelation 16. *match trumpets*

   1. Overview. Literal or symbolic? OT Roots. *Egypt + Babylon*

   7 in Egypt 2. *Plague 1—Sores/Boils.*

   #1 #16 3. *Plagues 2 and 3—Both are about water turning
      to blood.*

   #10 Death Curse God 4. *Plague 4—Sun scorches; no repentance or
      Creator worship.*

   9 Darkness 5. *Plague 5—Throne of the beast thrown into darkness.* *Demonic*

   Kings from E 6. *Plague 6—The "Battle of Armageddon"; Drying up the
      Euphrates River.*

   7. *Plague 7—Voice from the temple throne: "It is done."*

C. **More details about Babylon and its demise**—
Revelation 17-18.

   1. A great prostitute who sits by many waters.

   2. The fall of Babylon with a metaphor of economics.

   3. Babylon is fallen—same message, plus now: Come
      out of her!

D. **Summary Statement:** "Believe it: Babylon really does lose,
and it loses everything!"

Greek marturi witness testimony martyr

diak

not ¼ or ⅓ but entire earth

The Wrath of God

Does God ever get angry? It sure seems like it! Two Greek words get translated as "wrath" in Revelation. One is *thumos* which means anger or fury.

The other is *orge* which means righteous indignation and a demonstration of displeasure.

Both words get used interchangeably in Revelation to refer to God's final dealing with sin and Satan and all who are with him (see Revelation 14:19; 15:1; 15:7; 16:1).

To increase the intensity, both words get put together in Revelation 14:10; 16:19; 19:15.

You'll also find the "wrath of God" written about in Romans 1:18-25 and Romans 2:5-11.

Some Old Testament roots can be found in

> Exodus 15:7—"Song of Moses" reports God's anger
>
> Psalm 78:49—God unleashed his fury against Egypt
>
> Psalm 78:62—God was furious with his people
>
> Proverbs 11:23—The hope of the wicked ends in wrath
>
> Isaiah 13:9, 13—The Day of the Lord comes with wrath
>
> Jeremiah 7:29—God's people put under God's wrath
>
> Ezekiel 22:21-22—Jerusalem to receive God's wrath
>
> Ezekiel 38:19—God's wrath given to Gog
>
> Zephaniah 1:14-15—God's Day of Wrath on the earth

II Kings 8:10:11

John 15:

SESSION 8

Which Three Will You Believe?

Three Angels of Revelation 14	Three Frogs of Revelation 16
Angels = messengers from heaven	Frogs = unclean animals; Egyptian fertility god
Come from midair	Come from the mouths of the false trinity
Sent to the whole world	Go to the kings of the whole world
Proclaim the everlasting Gospel	Perform signs
Worship God, the Creator	Are demonic spirits
Babylon loses	Recruit for the fight against God Almighty
Babylon loses and won't return	

[handwritten note: Last thing false prophets could do ➝ ✓ moses,]

The plague of frogs in Egypt (Exodus 8:1-15) was the last plague Pharaoh's magicians were able to replicate and thus deceive Pharaoh into believing they could do everything Moses/God did.

A Thief in the Night?

Revelation 16:15

"Look, I come like a thief! Blessed is the one who stays awake and remains clothed, so as not to go naked and be shamefully exposed."

Revelation 3:3

[To the church in Sardis] "Remember, therefore, what you have received and heard; hold it fast, and repent. But if you do not wake up, I will come like a thief, and you will not know at what time I will come to you."

Matthew 24:42-44

"Therefore keep watch, because you do not know on what day your Lord will come. But understand this: if the owner of the house had known at what time of night the thief was coming, he would have kept watch and would not have let his house be broken into. So you also must be ready, because the Son of Man will come at an hour when you do not expect him."

Luke 12:35-40

"Be dressed ready for service and keep your lamps burning, like servants waiting for their master to return from a wedding banquet, so that when he comes and knocks they can immediately open the door for him. It will be good for those servants whose master finds them watching when he comes. Truly I tell you, he will dress himself to serve, will have them recline at the table and will come and wait on them. It will be good for those servants whose master finds them ready, even if he comes in the middle of the night or toward daybreak. But understand this: If the owner of the house had known at what hour the thief was coming, he would not have let his house be broken into. You also must be ready, because the Son of Man will come at an hour when you do not expect him."

2 Peter 3:10-12

"But the day of the Lord will come like a thief. The heavens will disappear with a roar, the elements will be destroyed by fire, and the earth and everything done in it will be laid bare. Since everything will be destroyed in this way, what kind of people ought you to be? You ought to live holy and godly lives as you look forward to the day of God and speed its coming."

1 Thessalonians 5:1-6

"Now, brothers and sisters, about times and dates we do not need to write to you, for you know very well that the day of the Lord will come like a thief in the night. While people are saying, 'Peace and safety,' destruction will come on them suddenly, as labor pains on a pregnant woman, and they will not escape. But you, brothers and sisters, are not in darkness so that this day should surprise you like a thief. You are all children of the light and children of the day. We do not belong to the night or to the darkness. So then, let us not be like others, who are asleep, but let us be awake and sober."

As children of God we are of Gods light. So no darkness for them.

Battle-of-armageddon.org

Armageddon

The term "Armageddon" occurs once in the entire Bible (Revelation 16:16). The Hebrew name is a compound word: har = mountain and megiddon = Megiddo.

Fortress of Megiddo

There is no "mountain of Megiddo" in the Old Testament, but there was a fortress city called Megiddo in Northern Israel. It was located on the Plain of Esdraelon, at the foot of Mount Carmel. This plain was a great highway from Egypt to Damascus.

Famous battles included:

- Deborah and Barak defeated Sisera and his army (Judges 5:19-21),
- King Ahaziah shot by Jehu (2 Kings 9:27),
- Pharaoh Necho killed King Josiah (2 Kings 23:29-30).

Mount Carmel Showdown

If the "Mountain of Megiddo" refers to Mount Carmel at the edge of the plain where the city of Megiddo stood, it brings to mind other Old Testament roots, primarily the showdown between Elijah and God against Ahab, Jezebel, and the false prophets of Baal (see 1 Kings 18).

Just as Elijah called down fire from heaven, the land beast (called the "false prophet" in Rev. 16:13) has imitated this by calling down fire from heaven to deceive others (see Rev. 13:13-14).

Battle for Jerusalem

In Zechariah 12, Jerusalem's enemies are to be destroyed. Verse 11 combines Megiddo with Jerusalem, and the weeping of Hadad Rimmon was mourning over the death of a pagan god's firstborn son (cf. Exodus 11:6; 12:29-31).

According to Daniel 2:35 and Daniel 11:45 the great mountain is God's kingdom arrayed against the kingdoms of this world.

That makes the "Mountain of Megiddo" the Jerusalem of major battles where God will defeat all his enemies.

SESSION 8

Seven Bowls/Plagues
Revelation 16

1. Sores/Boils—Revelation 16:2
Sixth Egyptian plague (Exodus 9:10-11)—This plague falls on those who have the mark of the beast and who worship the image to the beast. Having the mark of the beast on your skin (forehead or your hand) doesn't protect you from the sore/boils on your skin.

2. Sea turns to blood—Revelation 16:3
First Egyptian plague (Exodus 7:17-21)—Water, a source of life, results in death.

3. Rivers and springs of water turn to blood—Revelation 16:4
First Egyptian plague (Exodus 7:17-21)—In Egypt, turning the water to blood not only created a physical catastrophe but a challenge to Pharaoh, the god of the Nile, who claimed the ability to care for the Egyptians. Blood is given to those who shed blood.

4. Sun burns and scorches with fire—Revelation 16:8-9
Sun has been a key god throughout the ages. People now suffer from the very god they have worshiped and depended upon; and the water has already been turned to blood.

5. Throne of the beast thrown into darkness—Revelation 16:10-11
Ninth Egyptian plague (Exodus 10:21-23)—The power of the beast comes into question, and its authority erodes. Spiritual confusion and deception by the beast has given way to conscious and deliberate hatred of God.

6. Great River Euphrates is dried up—Revelation 16:12
Isaiah 44:24-28; Isaiah 45:1-7; Jeremiah 51:36-37—God dries up Euphrates to end Babylon and to "Make way for the kings from the East" (Isaiah 41:2; 46:11; 2 Chronicles 36:22-23).

7. <u>Voice from the temple throne, "It is done"—Revelation 16:17</u>
Babylon splits into three parts and then receives the cup of God's wrath followed by hailstones—seventh Egyptian plague (Exodus 9:24-25).

? *God goes back to heaven*

Which Woman?

Revelation 12 describes a woman in the wilderness who represents God's people. Revelation 17 describes a woman in the wilderness who gets named as Babylon. Both women can be found in the wilderness and both have some type of relationship with the dragon. The second woman counterfeits the first, but the differences are noteworthy.

Revelation 12 Woman	Revelation 17 Woman
Begins in the sky, surrounded by planets (vs. 1)	Begins on waters, surrounded by adulterous kings (vs. 1-2)
Attacked by the dragon (vs. 4, 13-17)	Resembles the dragon and attacks God's people (vs. 3, 6)
Escapes into exile (vs. 6)	Positioned like a queen (vs. 3-4)
Suffers alone in the wilderness (vs. 6, 14)	Prepares to party (vs. 4)
Cared for by God (vs. 6, 14)	Drunk from the blood of God's people (vs. 6)
Mother of the Messiah (vs. 5-6)	Mother of prostitutes (vs. 5)

Jerimiah 15.

Babylon name for false trinity
  Political, Kingdoms
  hills are mountains

The Seven Bowls/Plagues

Notes:

_____

_____

_____

_____

_____

_____

_____

_____

_____

_____

_____

_____

_____

_____

_____

_____

_____

_____

_____

_____

_____

SESSION 8

7, 5, 1 + 1, and an Eighth – Part 1

The confusing combinations in Revelation 17:8-11 can be placed into three sets (A, B, and C) that have four phases each. This may help to explain (or it may further confuse) the description.

Revelation 17:8—Set A has four phases

A1. The beast, which you saw, once was

A2. Now is not

A3. And yet will come up out of the Abyss

A4. And go to its destruction.

Revelation 17:10—Set B has four phases

B1. Five have fallen

B2. One is

B3. The other has not yet come

B4. But when he does come, he must remain for only a little while.

Revelation 17:11—Set C has four phases

C1. The beast who once was

C2. And now is not

C3. Is an eighth king. He belongs to the seven

C4. And is going to his destruction.

7, 5, 1 + 1, and an Eighth – Part 2

The three sets (A, B, C) of Revelation 17:8-11 can be viewed in their four phases by putting A1, B1, C1 into the first phase; then putting A2, B2, C2 into the second phase; then A3, B3, C3 into the third phase; and finally A4, B4, C4 into the fourth phase. It looks like this:

Phase 1—The beast of Revelation 17, also portrayed as the sea beast of Revelation 13:1-2, and the five kingdoms of Daniel 7.

    A1. The beast, which you saw, once was

        B1. Five have fallen

            C1. The beast who once was

Phase 2—a kingdom: Is it or isn't it? See Rev. 13:3 for what appears to be a fatal wound, but then is healed.

    A2. Now is not

        B2. One is

            C2. And now is not

Phase 3—comes from the Abyss after John's day; is an eighth king(dom) that comes from the seven-headed beast (Rev. 13:1-2; Dan. 7:7-14)

    A3. And yet will come up out of the Abyss

        B3. The other has not yet come

            C3. Is an eighth king. He belongs to the seven

Phase 4—the beast and its kingdoms lose quickly at the end (Rev. 17:11-14)

    A4. And go to its destruction

        B4. But when he does come, he must remain for only a little while

            C4. And is going to his destruction

No matter how you combine it, the devil, the beast, and the political and/or religious powers have been in charge of this planet for thousands of years. Their end will come, and it will happen quickly.

Summary Statement 5
Revelation 15:5-18:24

Believe it:
Babylon really does lose, and it loses everything!

Christ Conquers Sin Forever
Revelation 19:1-20:15

Basic Outline

Intro: Review seven bowls/plagues and the fall of Babylon. Babylon really does lose; and it loses everything!

A. **Introductory Sanctuary Scene:** Revelation 19:1-10. *Throne room of God*

Ps 104:35 4 Hallelujahs, 2 Suppers, and the testimony of Jesus. *Supernatural angel*
to praise God *From wedding to war*

B. **Here He comes**—Revelation 19:11-14.

1. Many Scriptural roots.

2. Crown—many *diadema*. *stephanos* Christ reigns on earth—finally! *Has won victory. Now real crown*

C. **The Second Supper**—Revelation 19:17-21.

1. Covenant curses of Deuteronomy 28:26; *God does us to be part of us.* Ezekiel 39:17-21. *Told in advance so we will know.*

2. No repentance; beast and false prophet cast into the lake of fire.

3. God's preparation for his bride includes cleansing the earth.

D. **The Millennium**—Revelation 20:1-15.

1. First section—Revelation 20:1-3: Satan bound to the Abyss.

2. Second section—Revelation 20:4-6. Thrones, judging. Then Life, death, two resurrections.

3. Third section—Rev. 20:7-10. Satan released; Gog and Magog; and "Tormented forever"

4. Fourth Section—Revelation 20:11-15. Earth destroyed; death thrown into the lake of fire.

E. **Summary Statement:** The enthronement of Jesus on earth brings about eternal justice: Hallelujahs for the righteous and final destruction for the wicked.

Hallelujah

You can find it 24 times in the Old Testament book of Psalms, but in the New Testament you'll find it only in Revelation 19, and then it appears four times. The word is actually a compound Hebrew word:

Halal = to praise

Yah = Yahweh, the name of God

Put it together and it simply means "Praise God"

The Four "Hallelujahs" of Revelation 19

1. God's judgments are right—Revelation 19:1-2

   - Babylon is condemned and the blood of God's servants finally is avenged.

   - Salvation is complete with the removal of the persecutors.

2. The smoke goes up from her forever—Revelation 19:3

   - Assurance that Babylon's demise is definite and irreversible.

3. Those in heaven worship and praise God—Revelation 19:4

   - Heaven joins the celebration regarding what God has done on earth.

4. God reigns—Revelation 19:6

   - On earth as it is in heaven.

Hebrew Wedding

Revelation 19:7— "The wedding of the Lamb has come, and his bride has made herself ready." Wedding metaphors have been used in other parts of the Bible. Jesus used them in his parables.

Mathew 22:2-14 (also in Luke 14:16-24)—invitations to God's wedding banquet

Matthew 25:1-13—wise and foolish bridesmaids when the bridegroom arrives

In the Old Testament, Israel is often described as a bride:

Isaiah 61:10—the year of God's favor is cause for rejoicing, like a bride.

Jeremiah 2:32—a bride wouldn't forget her wedding ornaments, but you have forgotten me!

Hosea 2:19-20—God promises to betroth his people to him forever.

A Hebrew wedding differed from Western weddings today. An ancient Hebrew wedding included these components:

1. Betrothal at the house of the bride's father and the groom pays the dowry. From this point on, they are considered to be husband and wife even though they are not yet living together. To break the engagement now requires a divorce.

2. The groom returns to his father's house to prepare a place for the groom and his bride.

3. The bride stays at her father's house and prepares herself for the wedding.

4. When both the place the groom has prepared for the bride is ready and the bride has prepared herself for the wedding, the bridegroom returns to the house of the bride's father to take her to his father's house, where the wedding will take place (see John 14:1-3).

Parallels between the Seven Seals and Christ Conquering Sin Forever

In Revelation 19:11, heaven stands open. Prior to this, a door had been opened into heaven (Revelation 4:1) and the temple in heaven had been open (Revelation 11:19; 15:5). But now all heaven opens and the armies of heaven come in full strength, not merely one rider at a time. With the parallel structure of the book of Revelation, "the seven seals" and "Christ Conquering Sin Forever" are in similar positions on opposite sides of the pyramid. Note the similarities.

Seven Seals	*Christ Conquers Sin Forever*
First Seal—white horse, crown, victory (6:2)	White horse, crowns, victory (19:11-13)
Second Seal—red horse, blood, war, sword (6:3-4)	Armies, blood, war, sword (19:14-16; 19-21)
Third Seal—Black horse, famine (6:5-6)	Feast of the dead (19:17-18; 21)
Fourth Seal—Pale horse, death (6:7-8)	From the Abyss/place of death (20:1-3)
Fifth Seal—Souls under the altar killed because of testimony wait in death (6:9-11)	Souls beheaded because of testimony come to life (20:4-6)
Sixth Seal—Battle of God's wrath (6:12-17)	Battle of Gog and Magog (20:7-10)
Seventh Seal—Silence, empty skies (8:1)	Great throne, heaven and earth empty (20:11-15)

Christ Conquers Sin Forever

Notes:

Think of Hebrew wedding

Fine linen was given her.

Baptism shows our commitment

In past God spoke to us by prophets   Joel 2:28,29

Outline of Revelation 20

Revelation 20:1-3

1. Satan bound and cast into the Abyss (bottomless pit) for 1,000 years

2. No deceiving the nations until the end of the 1,000 years
   Wicked are dead

3. Satan set free for a short time after the 1,000 years
   He will deceive nations again.

Revelation 20:4-6

1. Those given authority to judge are seated on thrones (Rev. 3:21)

2. This includes those martyred for God (Rev. 6:9-11)

3. Those faithful to God come to life and reign with Christ for 1,000 years

   Blessing for those who are part of this: the "first" resurrection
   The "second death" has no power over them
   They are priests of God and of Christ   *matt 7:1, 2*
   They reign with Christ for 1,000 years

4. The rest of the dead do not come to life until the 1,000 years are ended *wicked are reserected*

Revelation 20:7-10

1. Satan released from his prison after the 1,000 years (see Rev. 20:2)

2. Satan goes out to deceive the nations   *short Time*

3. Satan brings those deceived to battle against God and God's people

4. Fire comes down from heaven and devours Satan and those deceived

5. The devil is thrown into the lake of fire

Revelation 20:11-15

1. A great white throne with the One who rules the heavens and earth

2. Everyone stands before the throne

3. Books are opened

4. A book of Life is also opened

5. Judgment given based on what people have done, as recorded

6. Death and Hades are thrown into the lake of fire

7. The "lake of fire" is the second death

8. All who are not written in the book of life are thrown into the lake of fire

Three concepts that grabbed my attention in Revelation 20

1. Only the Blessed & Holy are raised & go to heaven.
   Key given to angel given back.
   Earth is purified x 2

2.

3.

Life and Death (and Death)

John mentions two kinds of life based on birth and the new birth. He also presents death as sleep and then a second death, which is final and eternal.

Life

The first kind of "life" occurs when a person is born. Jesus called this "born of water" when a woman's "water" breaks at the onset of the birthing process. This first birth is also called "born of the flesh."

The second kind of "life" is eternal life, which comes as a gift from God and can take place only after physical birth. This is called being "born again" or "born of the Spirit." Jesus told Nicodemus a person must be born of water (physical birth) and born of the Spirit (born again) in order to see the kingdom of God.

Eternal life begins NOW for those born of the Spirit (John 3:3-12; 5:24; 1 John 5:11-13).

First Death/Sleep (temporary)

"Death" on planet earth occurs when one's heart stops or breathing ceases due to accidents, physical attacks, health problems or old age. This can be referred to as the first death. It can terrify those who don't have the gift of eternal life. Jesus referred to this type of death as sleep (John 11:11-14).

John 5

Jesus resurrects all who experience this first death/sleep. Those faithful to God receive the "first resurrection" when Jesus returns and the millennium begins. Those who follow the dragon, beast and false prophet receive the "second resurrection" at the end of the millennium (see Rev. 20:4-6).

Second Death (eternal) 1 John 1: 11-13

The second death is eternal separation from God, who is the source of all life. Full and final destruction with no hope of return often gets described as fire or a lake of fire. Sometimes elements of "forever and ever" get added to indicate this is final. The second death will come to all who are not in the Lamb's "Book of Life" which also marks the end of death itself (see Rev. 20:10, 14-15).

Christ Conquers Sin Forever

Notes:

_____

_____

_____

_____

_____

_____

_____

_____

_____

_____

_____

_____

_____

_____

_____

_____

_____

_____

Resurrection

Some passages from John about "Resurrection":

John 5:24-29
"Very truly I tell you, whoever hears my word and believes him who sent me has eternal life and will not be judged but has crossed over from death to life. Very truly I tell you, a time is coming and has now come when the dead will hear the voice of the Son of God and those who hear will live. For as the Father has life in himself, so he has granted the Son also to have life in himself. And he has given him authority to judge because he is the Son of Man. Do not be amazed at this, for a time is coming when all who are in their graves will hear his voice and come out—those who have done what is good will rise to live, and those who have done what is evil will rise to be condemned."

John 6:40
"For my Father's will is that everyone who looks to the Son and believes in him shall have eternal life, and I will raise them up at the last day."

John 11:21-26
"Lord," Martha said to Jesus, "if you had been here, my brother would not have died. But I know that even now God will give you whatever you ask."

Jesus said to her, "Your brother will rise again."

Martha answered, "I know he will rise again in the resurrection at the last day."

Jesus said to her, "I am the resurrection and the life. The one who believes in me will live, even though they die; and whoever lives by believing in me will never die. Do you believe this?"

Revelation 20:6
"Blessed and holy are those who share in the first resurrection. The second death has no power over them, but they will be priests of God and of Christ and will reign with him for a thousand years."

Revelation 20:5
"The rest of the dead did not come to life until the thousand years were ended."

Revelation 20:14-15
"The lake of fire is the second death. Anyone whose name was not found written in the book of life was thrown into the lake of fire."

Why the Millennium Might Not Be 1,000 Years

Since the word "millennium" literally means "1,000 years" isn't that what it has to mean? The actual word "millennium" never appears in the Bible. It's a Latin word that does mean "1,000 years." The only place in the Bible 1,000 years appears is in Revelation 20 (five times).

But numbers in the symbolic book of Revelation usually represent qualities rather than quantities. The number 1,000 could symbolize:

- A military unit, like a battalion today

- An Israelite tribe

- A composite of 10 x 10 x 10 = 1,000
  When 10 = complete, and 3 = the unity of God, then 10 x 10 x 10 = complete unity
  When 10 = tested by trial and 3 = the unity of God, then 10 x 10 x 10 = tested by God

Because God's people will be judging during the 1,000 years the same types of things that those in heaven already judged (see Daniel 7:9-12), the literal amount of time is not the issue. The more important issue is that the "millennium" will take as long as is needed for all those redeemed to have all their questions answered about the justice of God—why certain people are in heaven and other people are not in heaven. It is vital to God that everyone in heaven, those redeemed from the earth, and even those who choose not to be redeemed from the earth have all their questions answered so the major question of God's justice (can God be trusted?) will be certain.

This has been predicted. "At the name of Jesus every knee will bow, in heaven and on earth and under the earth, and every tongue will confess that Jesus Christ is Lord, to the glory of God the Father (Philippians 2:10-11).

(See also Psalm 22:27; Psalm 66:4; Psalm 86:8-10; 1 Samuel 5:1-4; 1 Samuel 6:5; Isaiah 45:23; Daniel 4:37; Romans 14:10-13; Ephesians 1:10; Philippians 2:6-11; 1 Peter 3:22; Revelation 15:4.)

1 Tim 4

SESSION 9

Torment Forever

What does it mean when God torments forever the devil or the beast or the false prophet?

Basanizo is the Greek word usually translated as "torment" but that's not its first meaning. The word has at least two meanings:

1. a touchstone that tests metals to find what they are made of

2. torment or punishment

If you expect God to burn the wicked forever and ever, you would translate Revelation 20:10 as

> The beast and the false prophet will be tormented forever and ever.

If you don't expect God to burn the wicked forever and ever, you would translate Revelation 20:10 more like

> The beast and the false prophet will be tested and exposed for what they really are. There won't ever be a question about what they were really made of from this point on.

The same word appears in Revelation 12:2 and 14:10.

When Jesus cast out the demons, they shrieked, "Don't torment us" or "Don't show what we're really made of."

Another form of the same word can be found in Revelation 18:7; 18:10; 18:15; 14:11; 9:5.

"Tormenting forever" means that Satan has been tested and exposed forever—no more deception!

Basanizo
Mark 5:7

Tears are not wiped away til after millennium
I Cor 6:2-3

SESSION 9

Summary Statement 6
Revelation 19:1-20:15

- The enthronement of Jesus on earth brings about eternal justice

- Hallelujahs for the righteous

- Final destruction for the wicked

Ez 38-39

II Tim 2
1 Cor 13:12   15:20-25

Face-to-Face with Jesus
Revelation 21:1-22:21

Basic Outline

Intro: Review how Christ conquered sin forever from the previous session; Lots of "Hallalujahs"!

A. **Introductory Sanctuary Scene:** Revelation 21:1-8—Where is the sanctuary?

B. **Looking at the New Jerusalem**—Revelation 21:9-27.

   1. Comparing the New Jerusalem with Babylon.

   2. Descriptions of the two cities/women.

   3. Fate of the two cities/women.

C. **Moving Closer to the New Jerusalem in 7 steps**—Revelation 22:1-5.

D. **The Epilogue of the Book**—Revelation 22:6-21.

   1. Come.

   2. Are you an "Adventist"—someone anticipating Christ's coming?

   3. How do we live as we await the "soon" return of Jesus?

E. **A Few More Things**: John halted from angel worship; Do not seal up the words of the prophecy; polarization and continuity; seventh beatitude; water of life; grace.

F. **Summary Statement:** "Immanuel, Face-to-face."

"God will be with them and will be their God"

Some Old Testament roots for John's statement in Revelation 21:3:

Exodus 29:45-46
"Then I will dwell among the Israelites and be their God. They will know that I am the Lord their God, who brought them out of Egypt so that I might dwell among them. I am the Lord their God."

Leviticus 26:11-12
"I will put my dwelling place among you, and I will not abhor you. I will walk among you and be your God, and you will be my people. I am the Lord your God, who brought you out of Egypt so that you would no longer be slaves to the Egyptians. I broke the bars of your yoke and enabled you to walk with heads held high."

Jeremiah 24:7
"I will give them a heart to know me, that I am the Lord. They will be my people, and I will be their God, for they will return to me with all their heart."

Jeremiah 30:22
"So you will be my people, and I will be your God."

Jeremiah 32:38-41
"They will be my people, and I will be their God. I will give them singleness of heart and action, so that they will always fear me and that all will then go well for them and for their children after them. I will make an everlasting covenant with them. I will never stop doing good to them, and I will inspire them to fear me, so that they will never turn away from me. I will rejoice in doing them good and will assuredly plant them in this land with all my heart and soul."

Ezekiel 11:20
"Then they will follow my decrees and be careful to keep my laws. They will be my people, and I will be their God."

Ezekiel 37:23-27
"They will no longer defile themselves with their idols and vile images or with any of their offenses, for I will save them from all their sinful backsliding, and I will cleanse them. They will be my people, and I will be their God. My servant David will be king over them, and they will all have one shepherd. They will follow my laws and be careful to keep my decrees. They will live in the land I gave to my servant Jacob, the land where your ancestors lived. They and their children and their children's children will live there forever, and David my servant will be their prince forever. I will make a covenant of peace with them; it will be an everlasting covenant. I will establish them and increase their numbers, and I will put my sanctuary among them forever. My dwelling place will be with them; I will be their God, and they will be my people. Then the nations will know that I the Lord make Israel holy when my sanctuary is among them forever."

Ezekiel 43:7a
"He said, 'Son of man, this is the place of my throne and the place for the soles of my feet. This is where I will live among the Israelites forever.'"

Zechariah 13:9
"This third I will put into the fire; I will refine them like silver and test them like gold. They will call on my name and I will answer them; I will say, 'They are my people,' and they will say, 'The Lord is our God.'"

Two Sides of the Pyramid

In the pyramid structure of Revelation, the first part of the book and the last part of the book have several matching words or phrases.

First part of the book	*Last part of the book*
Christ is faithful and true (3:14)	God's words are faithful and true (21:5)
Jesus is the alpha and omega (1:8)	Jesus is the alpha and omega (21:6)
Jesus is the beginning and end (1:8)	Jesus is the beginning and end (21:6)
The overcomer receives promises (2:7, 11, 17, 26; 3:5, 12, 21)	The overcomer inherits these things (21:7)
God's face radiant like the sun (1:16)	The glory of God gives light (21:23)
Name of God on his people (3:12)	The Lamb's name on the foreheads (22:4)
Tree of life (2:7)	Tree of life (22:2)
Book of life (3:5)	The Lamb's book of life (21:27)
A loud voice like a trumpet (1:10)	A loud voice from the throne (21:3)
God present in the candlesticks (1:13)	God present in the New Jerusalem (21:1-8)
Victorious not hurt by the second death (2:11)	Second death to cowardly unbelievers and law breakers (21:8)
Overcomers sit on the throne (3:21)	Loud voice from the throne (21:3)
The New Jerusalem (3:12)	The New Jerusalem (21:3, 10)

In or Out?

In Revelation 21-22, John "sees" three perspectives. Each of these ends with those who receive what he sees in contrast to those who are excluded from this reward.

Revelation 21:1-8

John sees a new heaven and a new earth.

The recipients: Those who are victorious will inherit all this, and I will be their God and they will be my children.

Those excluded: But the cowardly, the unbelieving, the vile, the murderers, the sexually immoral, those who practice magic arts, the idolaters and all liars—they will be consigned to the fiery lake of burning sulfur. This is the second death.

Revelation 21:9-27

John sees the New Jerusalem.

The recipients: Those whose names are written in the Lamb's book of life.

Those excluded: Nothing impure will ever enter it, nor will anyone who does what is shameful or deceitful.

Revelation 22:1-15

John sees the river of life flowing from the throne.

The recipients: Blessed are those who wash their robes, that they may have the right to the tree of life and may go through the gates into the city.

Those excluded: Outside are the dogs, those who practice magic arts, the sexually immoral, the murderers, the idolaters and everyone who loves and practices falsehood.

Comparing Two Cities – 1

Note the similarities and differences between the settings for the descriptions of Babylon in Revelation 17 and of the New Jerusalem in Revelation 21.

The Setting for John's Visions

Babylon (Rev. 17:1-3)	New Jerusalem (Rev. 21:9-10)
One of the seven angels who had seven bowls	One of the seven angels who had seven bowls full of the seven last plagues
Came and spoke with me saying	Came and spoke with me saying
Come here, I will show you…	Come, I will show you
the great prostitute…	the bride,
with whom the kings of the earth have committed fornication	the wife of the Lamb
and he carried me away in the Spirit	and he carried me away in the Spirit
into a wilderness	to a great and high mount
And I saw	and showed me
the great city (17:18)	the holy city,
Babylon (17:5)	Jerusalem
Sitting on many waters	descending out of heaven
on a scarlet beast	from God

Adapted from Ranko Stefanovic's *Revelation of Jesus Christ.*

Comparing Two Cities – 2

Note the similarities and differences between the descriptions of Babylon in Revelation 17 and of the New Jerusalem in Revelation 21 and 22.

The Descriptions of the Two Cities/Women

Babylon	New Jerusalem
The woman was dressed in purple and scarlet, and was glittering with gold, precious stones and pearls (17:4).	It shone with the glory of God, and its brilliance was like that of a very precious jewel, like a jasper, clear as crystal (21:11).
She held a golden cup in her hand, filled with abominable things and the filth of her adulteries (17:4).	the river of the water of life, as clear as crystal, flowing from the throne of God (22:1).
a dwelling for demons (18:2).	God's dwelling place is now among the people, and he will dwell with them (21:3).
a haunt for every unclean spirit (18:2).	Nothing impure will ever enter it (21:27).
every unclean bird, every unclean and detestable animal (18:2).	nor will anyone who does what is shameful or deceitful (21:27).
The inhabitants of the earth whose names have not been written in the book of life from the creation of the world will be astonished when they see the beast (17:8).	but only those whose names are written in the Lamb's book of life (21:27).
Peoples, multitudes, nations and languages (17:15).	The nations and the kings (21:24).
Will give their power and authority to the beast (17:13).	will bring their splendor into it (21:24).

Adapted from Ranko Stefanovic's *Revelation of Jesus Christ.*

Comparing Two Cities – 3

Note the similarities and differences between the fate of Babylon in Revelation 16 and 18 and of the New Jerusalem in Revelation 21 and 22.

The Fate of the Two Cities

Babylon	New Jerusalem
It is done (16:17)	It is done (21:6)
God will give to Babylon the cup of the wine of fury of his wrath (16:19)	God will give freely to the thirsty from the fountain of the water of Life (21:6)
In one day her plagues will come, death and mourning and famine, and she shall be burned with fire (18:8)	And no longer shall there be death, neither sorrow… nor pain (21:4)
The light of a lamp will never shine in you any longer (18:23)	The Lamb is its lamp; the nations will walk by its light (21:23-24); the Lord will illumine them (22:5)
Babylon adorned with gold and precious stones and pearls is brought to ruin (18:16-17)	Jerusalem has the glory of God. Her brilliance was like a precious stone, like a jasper stone sparkling (21:11)
Babylon reigns as a queen, but with her inhabitants she is doomed to destruction (18:7-8)	The throne of God and of the Lamb will be in it, and his servants will serve him (22:3)
Babylon is thrown down with violence and will never be found any longer (18:21)	The Lord God shall illumine them; they will reign forever and ever (22:5)

Adapted from Ranko Stefanovic's *Revelation of Jesus Christ*.

Marvels of the New Jerusalem

John's description of the New Jerusalem starts from a distance and moves closer and closer until he eventually reaches the heart of the city. Each description provides yet another marvel. These can be listed in seven stages. Each creates additional marvels for the observer. These are found in Revelation 21:10-22:5.

1. The city as a whole, brilliantly shining like a precious jewel, clear as crystal

2. The gates of pearl and walls and foundation of precious stones, also shining brilliantly

3. The main square of gold, like transparent glass

4. The river of the water of life, also clear as crystal

5. On each side of the river, the tree of life bearing fruit and providing healing leaves for all

6. The throne of God and the Lamb

7. The Lord God Himself—we will see his face and his name will be on our foreheads.

Prologue and Epilogue

The book of Revelation has a prologue and epilogue that match, providing balance, emphasis, and focus. Here are some of the matching elements in the prologue and epilogue of Revelation, as well as a major message.

Prologue	*Epilogue*
The revelation from Jesus Christ, which God gave him to show his servants what must soon take place. He made it known by sending his angel (1:1)	The angel gave a trustworthy and true message to show his servants the things that must soon take place (22:6)
Blessed is the one who reads, hears, and takes this to heart because the time is near (1:3)	Blessed are those who hear and keep the words of this prophecy; the time is near (22:7-10)
Greetings to the churches (1:4-6)	I give you this testimony for the churches (22:16)

Major Message

Prologue	*Epilogue*
"From him who is…to *come*" (1:4)	"Look, I am *coming* soon!" (22:7)
"Look, he is *coming*" (1:7)	"Look, I am *coming* soon!" (22:12)
"The Lord, who is…to *come*" (1:8)	"The Spirit and bride say 'Come!' (22:17)
	"Let the one who hears say 'Come!'" (22:17)
	"Let the one who is thirsty come" (22:17)
	"Yes, I am *coming* soon" (22:20)
	"*Come*, Lord Jesus" (22:20)

Summary Statement 7
Revelation 21:1-22:21

Immanuel; Face-to-face

Introductory Sanctuary Scenes

Following are the seven Sanctuary Scenes that introduce the seven portions of Revelation

- **Introductory Sanctuary Scene 1—Seven Churches (Rev. 1:9-20)**
  Jesus walks among the seven candlesticks indicating that he is present with his people on earth

- **Introductory Sanctuary Scene 2—Seven Seals (Rev. 4-5)**
  Jesus enthroned with exuberant celebration in heaven. Jesus, the victorious Lamb, is worthy to open the seals

- **Introductory Sanctuary Scene 3—Seven Trumpets (Rev. 8:2-5)**
  Censer of prayers thrown to the earth, calling God's people to come for daily prayer

- **Introductory Sanctuary Scene 4—The Heart of the Book (Rev. 11:19)**
  God Himself, with the covenant relationship motif

- **Introductory Sanctuary Scene 5—Seven Last Bowls/ Plagues (Rev. 15:5-8)**
  God on his throne responds to the testimony of his martyrs

- **Introductory Sanctuary Scene 6—Christ Conquers Sin Forever (Rev. 19:1-10)**
  Heaven erupts in Hallalujahs because sin comes to an end on earth

- **Introductory Sanctuary Scene 7—New Jerusalem (Rev. 21:2-8)**
  God is with his people in person so there's no need for another sanctuary

Revelation 101 Summaries

*Following are the seven summaries from the
seven portions of Revelation*

- **Summary 1—Revelation 1:1-3:22**
  Immanuel

- **Summary 2—Revelation 4:1-8:1**
  Take heaven's perspective and follow the Lamb
  instead of the world

- **Summary 3—Revelation 8:2-11:18**
  God warns with wrath and mercy as he listens for
  prayers and looks for repentance

- **Summary 4—Revelation 11:19-15:4**
  Will you worship the True Trinity or the false trinity?
  Worship of the True Trinity will requires an enduring
  trust in Jesus

- **Summary 5—Revelation 15:5-18:24**
  Believe it: Babylon really does lose, and it loses
  everything!

- **Summary 6—Revelation 19:1-20:15**
  The enthronement of Jesus on earth brings about
  eternal justice: Hallelujahs for the righteous and final
  destruction for the wicked

- **Summary 7—Revelation 21:1-22:21**
  Immanuel; Face-to-face